Best wishes

Carol McCall

September,
2000

Listen! There's a World Waiting to Be Heard

Listen! There's a World Waiting to Be Heard

The Empowerment of Listening

Carol McCall

VANTAGE PRESS
New York

FIRST EDITION

Copyright © 2000 by Carol McCall

Published by Vantage Press, Inc.
516 West 34th Street, New York, New York 10001

Manufactured in the United States of America
ISBN: 0-533-13115-4

Library of Congress Catalog Card No.: 99-93677

0 9 8 7 6 5 4 3 2 1

Contents

Preface

Next to breathing, listening is the single most important thing you and I do. Yet, did you know that most people only listen at 25 percent of their capacity? Imagine for jut a moment what would be possible for you—in all of your relationships, in your work, your family, in every area of your life—if you could improve your ability to really listen by as a little as ten percent more than you do now. That's the opportunity you have by reading this book.

The genesis of this book occurred in a conversation I had with a close associate and friend, John Fogg. John is a contributing editor for *Success* magazine and owns Upline Publishing, based in Charlottesville, Virginia. We originally produced an audio tape of our conversation, which has been used by thousands of people to enhance their ability to listen to one another. Since so many people have received so much value from the audio tape, it was decided to create a book that would allow me to share what I have learned with even greater numbers of people.

There is something special about a book. Reading stimulates different senses. It also allows the readers to proceed at whatever pace they wish, pausing whenever they want to ponder an idea or dwell on any thought.

Since this book is about listening, we decided to stay with the conversation format, in which John and I take turns speaking and listening to each other.

My personal wish is that you the reader become one of the "masterful listeners" given that "there's a world waiting to be heard!"

Acknowledgments

I wish to acknowledge God, my mother Lucy, my husband Noldy, my son Raleigh, my daughter Ana, John Fogg, Richard Brooke, and the thousands of people who have so generously supported me and joined in my world vision of 100 million masterful listeners by the year 2020.

Listen! There's a World Waiting to Be Heard

One

What Passes For Listening in the Twentieth Century

Carol McCall, creator and leader of the Empowerment of Listening course, and her friend and associate John Fogg, contributing editor for Success Magazine, *sit together preparing to have a conversation about listening and the power that is created for all parties engaged in dialogue when real listening occurs. John speaks first:*

John: Carol, my dictionary says that to listen is to make an effort to hear something, to pay attention. Is that the meaning of listening for you?

Carol: Listening is more than paying attention. It's paying attention to the speaker with nothing else going on in your mind. Not as in "I'm listening to you and I'm thinking about what I'm going to do next." We're going to talk about paying heed with total concentration on the person speaking.

John: Why does that matter?

Carol: When you pay close attention to the person speaking, a very interesting thing happens. The other person begins to experience, for the first time maybe, being heard, having someone's total attention. By the time people are two, three, maybe five years old, they have unfortunately been socialized not to expect Mommy or Daddy or the adult world to give them full attention. So when you really pay attention to someone it begins to start a process of complete exchange in communication, a complete energy exchange. Not having any background thoughts, not having any noise going on in your head, allows you to be totally present with someone. It also allows you to enter into a sort of meditative state so that people experience being heard. It's a brand new experience for most people.

John: What's the value for me if you're really hearing me?

Carol: The fact that I've paid attention to you, that I've really heard you, puts you at ease and allows you to start relaxing. Also, there's an "unconditionality" about the listening I'm talking about. You'll feel that I'm not going to change you, I'm not trying to adjust you, I'm not going to give you any additions or do any subtractions to who you are as the speaker. Since I'm listening to you, you are fully able to express yourself because I'm interested and I'm not going to interfere with your communication.

Listening opens up the space for anything to come out of the conversation, even things that you weren't aware of. You'll begin to speak about things that will make you say, "Where did that come from? I didn't know I felt that way." Because when listening occurs without the residual conversation in one's head, what I call "empathic listening," the speaker begins to speak from their depth, from their history. They begin to speak from many, many past experiences. The total person comes forward.

John: How is that different from how we usually listen and speak with each other?

Carol: How we usually listen and speak with each other is you ask me a question and I'll give you an answer. You're waiting for me to finish so you can give me a rebuttal or a correction to what I said, an addition to what I said, a comment about what I said, a "one-up" about what I said. It's like a Ping-Pong game. I'm not really listening. I'm just waiting for your serve. So you serve, I serve and then we're not listening. It's more combative.

John: When I'm considering what I'm going to say next, I stop listening to you. I'm now paying attention to what I'm going to say. It seems to me that when I operate that way the conversation's all about me!

Carol: Yes. The conversation is about you when you operate that way. With empathic listening the conversation is about the person speaking and you, the listener, are fully aligned and in partnership with the person speaking.

John: So one of the results, obviously, is a much cleaner, clearer, and deeper sense of relationship.

Carol: Yes, that is what happens. Trust begins to happen, and intimacy—a form of intimacy that most people are capable of but think that they are afraid of. This intimacy goes beyond what most people think of as touchy-feely or too much involvement. With this type of listening you are involved, and there's no long-term involvement. You don't have to sign up for life. Listening provides an instant five-second human contact, a human understanding and appreciation. Then we're done.

John: It sounds passive. Is it?

Carol: Not at all. To pay that kind of full attention, you need to be present. You need to be active. You need to cut off the background listening in your head. You need to stop thinking about, "Did you balance your checkbook? Did the kids get to school on time? What about the grocery list? What about getting the car fixed?"

You've got to turn all of that off. This means you have to be very active in your listening. To be fully present requires that you pay attention and make eye contact if that's what works for you. If not, listen intently with both ears to really hear what the person has to say. And one more thing: you need to trust that you can listen intuitively—to listen internally—to what that person is saying. It's almost like walking in the other person's shoes. There's nothing passive about it at all. When people listen like this, they will experience some weariness. They will get tired.

John: Then listening is hard work?

Carol: Yes, real listening is hard work. In the initial stages, most people quit. They decide that it's too hard. However, for those people who hang in and give real listening, the rewards are remarkable. People around them get well. People around them develop. They become productive. They become profitable. They fulfill their dreams. And all because of the listening.

John: There's a part of this that's a little hard to believe. I think most of us think that it's in the speaking that we are creative. It's in the speaking that we're taking action. You're saying it's in the listening that creativity is happening.

Carol: I am saying that. And when a person is heard, their speaking is more focused on having their lives go the way they want them to. When we speak we create our present and our future. Listening facilitates the speaking so that there's more accuracy in it, more directness. When you're heard, you speak that which is important to you, that which is dear to you, that which is the way you will design your life. When you're not heard, you fumble around for what you want to say. You speak with uncertainty. You speak with "un-clarity." A lot of times, our lives look very chaotic because we haven't been heard. But once we are heard, clarity sets in and we speak our truth.

John: Let me go back to this dialogue in our head, this chatter. Give me some examples of the kinds of things that stand in the way of our listening. How can people tell when they're doing this?

Carol: Some people listen with skepticism, like "Yeah, well whatever, okay." Or maybe, "Yeah, I've seen that. I've been there. I've done that one. I already know this."

This kind of listening stifles the speaker because they're speaking into a listening that stops them or stops their ability to truly communicate what's so for them. Have you ever been around people you wanted to have a conversation with and you felt stifled, like whatever you said you felt cut off? Even if they didn't cut you off, you cut yourself off because it was like you were trying to prove something to them. The reason you have that experience is because they're not listening to you. They have that internal chatter going on.

John: I don't say to myself, "I'm not being heard here." I make another assessment that's far more damning. It's "This person doesn't care. I'm not interesting to this person." Or "I'm boring" or "This person is boring." What comes up right away is a negative judgment about myself or about the other person and it always ends with my going away.

What other background noises can stand in the way, Carol, besides the "I already know that"?

Carol: Some other things that get communicated are, "Prove it to me." "Show me." "What are you up to?" "Come on and get to the bottom line." Or "I'm not going to be emotional about this." When that happens, most of us, whether we're the speaker or the listener, have no idea what's going on. As you said, John, we think, "That person doesn't like me, they're not interested, what's wrong with me?" If you're thinking that, it's a very good clue that the other person is not really listening to you.

John: Wouldn't it also follow that if I was thinking there's something wrong with them, that would be a clue that I'm not listening?

Carol: That would be the same thing, yes.

John: So, any judgmental conclusion indicates that I'm not listening.

Carol: That's it exactly. Any time you're judgmental, or you want to have a rebuttal, you're not truly listening.

John: Now I know why you say it's hard work.

Carol: When you're non-judgmental, there's clarity between the two of you. There's nothing extra going on. The speaker will relax, knowing that the listener is giving him or her their undivided "listening."

John: Simply being present and wide open?

Carol: Yes.

John: What is the distinction you make between listening and thought? As you speak about the things that prevent us from listening wide open, it sounds like they're the thoughts we're having.

Carol: Yes. You have thoughts going through your mind all the time. The listening state to achieve is that place where you diminish the background thoughts and really train yourself to have one consistent thought, which is: "This person has value." That can mean "This person is interesting" or "This person is a leader" or "This person is capable." All other thoughts you work to get out of your head. That's why I say listening is not passive. If you find yourself straying, you focus your attention on the person. Whatever thought comes up other than "This person is interesting, this person is capable, this person is a leader," you get rid of. You're very pro-active in this process. That's why it's work.

Now, here's the good news. After a while you don't have to do that much work because you've trained yourself to listen to people a certain way. It's like a paradigm shift in your reactions to people. Out of that shift, listening begins to be very fluid for you. It does take practice to get there, however.

John: It sounds like you're programming yourself to listen in a more open, nonattached way.

Carol: That's a good word, nonattached. It doesn't matter what they say really. That they are heard is what really matters. That's what frees them up. That's what liberates them to go do what they want in their life. John, you know one of the things that all of us want is to be accepted. Really being heard provides unconditional acceptance. The listener is saying, "Who you are is valuable, so what you say is valuable. It's worth hearing. I may not agree with it and that doesn't matter. I don't have to agree in order to listen to you."

John: Wait a minute. You don't have to agree?

Carol: That's right.

John: In trying to remember all of the conversations of my life right now, I recall that they so often fall into "agree" or "disagree." When I disagree with someone, I find that to be disagreeable. What am I up to there? What am I doing in my listening?

Carol: You are evaluating, judging, weighing whether or not their particular paradigm fits yours and if it's going to affect your life in any way. In authentic listening that's not necessary. The two of you have joined together and you're communicating that "I'm listening to you. You're going to show me how you see things. You're going to demonstrate to me how you perceive life and how you want to go through life. I'm looking at it with you as a nonattached observer. It's like a research project for both of us. I'm there simply to see what you have. You're showing me your wares, so to speak. I don't have to agree with your paradigm. I simply need to listen."

When I disagree with something, I think my paradigm is being threatened. That's what usually happens with a disagreement.

8

John: So it's "I'm right and you're wrong?"

Carol: Yes. We don't see that we're both right at the same time. Your paradigm is right for you; my paradigm is right for me. We just see it differently. You've heard those stories about a car accident: thirty-five people standing around who saw the same accident and no two people tell the same story about what happened. No two people have the same perspective because they have different paradigms for seeing things.

John: Where is truth in all of this?

Carol: Oh, that's a great question, John. When you listen unconditionally without judgment and criticism, you will hear a person's truth. Truth is moment to moment to moment—what is so for that person *right now*. I'm not talking about the ultimate universal truth. I'm talking about what's true in that moment. I have a headache now; right now that's true.

If I say I have a headache, what I want you to get is that I'm uncomfortable right now. That's how I want you to listen to me. Don't fix it. Don't try to persuade me that I don't have a headache. Some people will say, "You don't have a headache; you're just trying to figure out something." Or "You should have done this" or "You're tired."

When you really listen to a person who has a headache, you get it. You simply get the communication. That's what's so for them in that moment. That's their truth. Because you haven't tried to fix it, you have entered into a partnership with them that will allow *them* to get rid of the headache, because now they can relax and be at ease with what's so for *them* in the moment and take the necessary actions. They can let their mind wander to "Maybe I took some kind of medication that gave me a headache" or "It could be that I'm tired." "It could be that I slept on the pillow wrong." "Maybe I have something too tight on my head." They can trace it back to the source because they've been heard.

I know it sounds strange—how can you have that happen just by listening? I say you can. You absolutely can. Listening is one of the most powerful tools in communication, and it is given the least credit. It's actually the nucleus of real communication. We need to be powerful listeners, not speakers, because when we listen, we will be powerful speakers. We usually think it's the other way around. We've got it reversed.

John: A lot of what you're saying is going in the direction of what I know as meditation—clearing the mind, emptying the mind. As I've involved myself with spiritual practices, one of things I found almost impossible to do is to stop my thinking, to clear my mind. As I recall, in this conversation, you said that that's not a goal, that what I want to do is replace those critical thoughts with something that is more—more what? More empowering?

Carol: Yes. In the meditative state, many people chant. They do mantras. It's like a constant repeated praying to get rid of the other thoughts that are going through their minds. The empowerment of listening is similar but different. I'm not asking you to chant a phrase in your head. I am asking, though, that you hold the thought that this person is capable, that this person is to be respected, that this person is valuable, that this person is a leader. Hold the thought of affinity. "I am in affinity with this person. I am here to partner with this person." Hold these thoughts. They allow the unconditionality of your listening to emerge. They allow the person to continue to speak because you're not putting up any resistance. And as they keep speaking, they get more and more and more powerful in your presence.

John: So, I can listen to someone as a jerk, and I can listen to someone as a leader? Are you really saying that's how they're going to show up?

Carol: That's exactly how they're going to show up. You see, I can listen to a leader, someone who's been proclaimed as a leader in our society, and hold them as a jerk. I listen to that person as though they're a jerk. Everything that comes out of their mouth is a stupid thing to say. "Wow, what a jerk!" I will miss any gems of wisdom. Because of the way I listen to that person, I will miss anything that will be of value to my life. I can't hear anything of importance that they have to say. All of my listening is directed toward that person so they show up like a jerk. I'll look for all the faults in that person, all the errors they make because I've already determined they're a jerk.

When I listen to someone as though they're a leader, what I will see are their strengths, the things they've accomplished. What I will see in their actions are the things that they fulfill and deliver on for all of us, that benefit everybody. I will listen for their value. I will listen for a contribution because I've already determined that they're a leader. That's how this process works. That's what listening does. What's important is for us to catch the listening that we have for people—those thoughts that are constantly going through our minds. We have them about everybody. They're called opinions. People tend to get rigid with their opinions. They think, "My opinion is who I am." Not so. You are far more than your opinions and opinions can be changed. You can change an opinion by changing your listening.

John: If you've been with a person for five years, ten years, fifteen years, you probably have a set type of listening for him or for her. That's a pretty wonderful state. Do we literally keep or create our relationships at the level they are by how we're listening?

Carol: Yes, we do. We've developed these opinions early in our relationships. They may have seemed small at the time, but they've affected us. We all have a habit of saying, "Well, it wasn't that big a deal." Oh, yes, it was! It was a big deal because out of that we formed an opinion, i.e., a *type* of listening for that person early in the relationship. If they forgot to call us and told us they were coming home thirty minutes late, we decided they can't be counted on. They lied. They don't love me. They just don't think I'm important. Fleeting as these opinions may be, they become a kind of listening we have for that person. That person could spend the next twenty or thirty years trying to prove to us that they love us. We make them prove it because of that one night—that one incident. We continue to look for evidence to support our opinions. The next time they come in five minutes late—see! The next time they come in an hour late—see! We keep looking for evidence because we've already designed a listening about that person.

John: Why do we do that?

Carol: There's fear in being authentic with someone we love. We're socialized to feel that if you let somebody know how much you really care about them, they're going to hurt you. We're taught very early not to show our feelings. Men in particular; women are called "over-emotional." So when we turn around and tell the truth, such as "I'm really sad you

12

came home late because I was excited and I was anticipating your coming home," we feel that person is probably going to turn around and hurt us. Usually we don't have the courage to say that.

John: Even if we do counseling, or through transformational or personal development work, we learn a new thing to say, that listening is probably still in place.

Carol: Exactly. Because usually when we do transformational work, listening is not addressed. This whole technology around listening is very new. It not only addresses how people listen in terms of their opinions and their thoughts, it also brings in intuition. It's in your intuitive listening that you hear a lot of answers. We know a lot of things about people intuitively. We ignore them. We don't pay attention to them.

John: True. But I have trouble separating what is a thought or imagination and what is intuition. I'll climb on an airplane, for example, and my marvelously creative mind will bring up a picture of the wheel falling off on takeoff and the plane skidding off the runway. Is that intuitive or just imaginative? How do I know the difference?

Carol: That's a question that many people ask and there is a very fine line between your mind playing with you and your intuition. When it's intuitive, there is a surge, like a charge. It's almost like a electrical current that goes through the body, like you get it. You know it. When you get something intuitively, it's definitive. When it's your mind, your logic or your imagination, you play with it. "Well, maybe it is and maybe it isn't." Your mind can conjure up emotions—it does that. However, with intuition it's a solid "klunk!" You don't question it. Now you may ignore it. And you can say later that you knew that it was so. Because we haven't trained ourselves intuitively, we haven't paid attention intuitively, the "still small voice" is still very small. It's very quiet. However, when you start to live from your intuition and pay attention to that small voice, it gets loud and your body starts to go with your intuition. It feels like there's a resolution. It comes like a total experience. Sight, smell, sound, taste, touch, hearing, all are included in your intuition.

John: You described intuition almost like it's a done deal. When I have something intuitive, it's complete—distinct from the times when I notice my thought or image is always fussing, never ending, not resolved. So is that a way that I can distinguish between my intuition and my imagination?

Carol: Yes, it is. And it can be a difficult distinction because we're so well-trained logically that our mind comes in immediately, sometimes even masquerading as intuition. It will appear in a nanosecond. In the early stages of training yourself to be a masterful listener, you'll need to pay close attention. You'll need to train yourself to pay attention to that first burst of energy, before the mind comes in. After a while, you'll get the distinction between the two.

John: Are there things we can do to create our own personal training programs, so to speak, to be able to recognize that intuition?

Carol: Yes. And you'll need to take some risks. You'll need to trust something that you have an intuition about. Start by intuiting where something is, who's on the phone, who's at the door.

John: Tell me how.

Carol: Suppose the phone rings. You say, "That's probably Roger."

John: Before picking up the phone, what do I do? How do I get to thinking that it's probably Roger?

Carol: There will be a very small, quiet answer. Not in your head, but something you feel within your body. And within your body, a name will come. It won't feel like an answer. It won't feel like a word. It's something you'll just *know*; this is Roger. You pick up the phone and there's Roger. And sometimes it won't be Roger. It might be Jane. It might be Harry. Keep playing with it. Be willing to take the risk to see. More times than not, you'll be right.

John: The notion of risk disappears for me when you say "play." Most of the time when I'm playing, I'm not risking a whole lot. It's not like professional sports where my career or life is on the line. But *playing* with it, for me at least, opens up some access to finding out what's going on. Maybe I could open a book randomly to a page and *play* first with what might be written there.

Carol: Yes, yes. Play with, "I want some information about how best to increase my business. This page is going to give me that piece of information." Then open the book and look to see if that page doesn't give you that information. When you start to play with your intuition, you'll discover that it is always on. It's never off. We are off when we don't pay attention to it.

15

John: When I've heard that idea before—that if you just open a book to any page the lesson will be there for you—I've thought that, if it worked, it was just coincidence.

Carol: Very often people who are logical—and most of us live in our logical, left brain—think that if there's not a rational reason, if we don't have the step by step by step proof, then it was a coincidence. But many things in our listening and intuition are not coincidences. They are direct communications from the world we live in. Children come here hearing everything. They don't miss anything. And they're not yet logical. They move with intuition and spontaneity. Children wear adults out because we're so busy being logical while they are being intuitive and spontaneous.

John: Is spontaneous always intuitive?

Carol: I'm still doing research about that. I know that there is a controversy about whether intuition and spontaneity go together. As far as I can tell, they do. And I'm open to discovering whether that's so.

John: Two questions come to mind right away. What relationship, if any, does intuition have with gender? I know I was brought up to hear about a "woman's intuition." I don't think I ever heard anything about a man's intuition. The other question is, since we had intuition as children, how did we stop having it? Is it biological? Did our educational system beat it out of us?

Carol: Let me start with the children question. From our earliest years, we're told what we should do. Our parents, who want us to fit with the morals and customs of our society, train us with a lot of dos and don'ts, stops, shoulds, shouldn'ts, etc. By the time a child is five, they no longer trust their intuition because they've been told what they *can't* do, what they *can* do, what they *should* do, and what they *shouldn't* do. So they don't listen to the still, small voice. The closest they come to it is the little imaginary friends they have. They have little monsters and lions, little bears, little birds. They talk to all kinds of imaginary playmates. This is as close to their intuition as they can be. When they get to school, it's amazing: their creativity and spontaneity are regimented so that they cease to be creative, intuitive thinkers.

There is no room in the rules and regulations for us to be creative, for us to be intuitive. We can't use our intuition about what's right and wrong for us in that moment. These are the rules. These are the regulations. This is what you follow.

John: In school we're given answers instead of finding answers. Is that what you're speaking about?

Carol: That's everything I'm talking about. We become critical thinkers, trained to start from, "Given the information, given the hypothesis, given the theme, given the thesis, then this is what must be so." But seldom are we raised or trained to think, "Given these parameters within which to work, what do I sense? What do I intuit about this?" Nobody does that not in the overall educational system. Maybe the Montessori schools, or Waldorf schools that are very committed to the education of the total child, are doing more of these intuitive studies, but not our general education system.

John: I know that you spent time professionally as an educator, especially in schools. Isn't there far more emphasis on the logic of math and science than on art or music?

Carol: Yes, there is. One of the first programs to be cut out will be the fine arts; music, choir, art, drama, where you have to use your intuition. In theater, for example, you have to intuit the part that you're playing, even if you have a script.

John: You know, there seems to be a big difference between facing an equation or problem that must be "solved" and facing a blank canvas or the raw lump of clay that you need to shape into something. There are two totally different behaviors involved and different mental and emotional processes involved.

Carol: One is given a much heavier weight than the other, and that is the left brain where our logic, our thinking, our reading, our processing takes place. By the time we finish school, we're all very skilled in our logic and our thinking. We're quite disabled in terms of our creativity and our intuition.

John: How does this show up in our listening? Do we have a listening for numbers or science but not a listening for creativity?

Carol: We don't think that creativity is substantial. You can't *prove* creativity, and we're raised in a society where you have to *prove* everything. When we're listening to someone's point of view, we're listening for whether or not they'll *prove* it.

You know, show me the facts. Get to the bottom line. Cut to the chase.

John: That comes down to right and wrong again.

Carol: Yes, it does. And we're trained that way.

John: I was schooled as an artist. I have a Bachelor of Fine Arts degree, so I'm particularly sensitive to this. Right/wrong doesn't live in art like it does in science or in some other logical field.

Carol: Yes, that's accurate. But here's the good news. Finally, the quantum physicists are moving in the direction of "both-and"—like the observed behavior of particles and waves are both "correct," depending upon the way they are observed. Now *you* can have a perspective, *I* can have a perspective, and they're *both* accurate. This seeming paradox is closer to what you're talking about in terms of art. There is no right art or wrong art. There's art—and either you like it or you don't.

I'm so thrilled that this new approach is happening, coming into the twenty-first century. It's recent, within this last decade, so I don't know how long it's going to take to become part of our culture. I know that when we start to listen to people and hold them as "right" for what they're saying, we are really moving in that direction. That immediately creates a partnership. We can build organizations with 70 to 80 thousand people in them who are working from their hearts. They're working from their intuition, and they're bringing in logic.

I don't ever want to imply that I don't believe in logic. You definitely need logic. You need to prove things. Come from your intuition and back it up with logic. Starting with logic to prove that the intuition is right is backwards. Even Einstein intuited the theory of relativity and then he proved it.

John: Carol, let's go back to that gender question. Does one particular sex use intuition better, have greater access to it?

Carol: I think that's one of our myths about communication. Boys aren't supposed to be emotional and girls are *too* emotional. The idea that girls can't do math as well as boys is part of that myth. It's not true. Men as well as women have intuition. Einstein is only one example of a man using his intuition in a powerful way. A woman has more permission in our culture to use her intuition. Men follow "hunches" or "gut feel" and that's okay. If it's called intuition, they'll likely ignore it. Some of our most wealthy and powerful men, and some of our greatest generals, admit to following hunches. What they do is use the brilliance of their intuition followed by their logic. And they do it so quickly that it appears that they are brilliant thinkers.

John: So, intuition and thinking are two different things?

Carol: They are two different things and they come from two separate domains. Research indicates that intuition and the thinking process are closely linked and they come within a nanosecond of each other. It's almost like a camera: you see the picture and then you take the picture. The challenge lies in recognizing intuition, that first nanosecond.

John: The only place I've seen intuition discussed is in transformational management and leadership material. In developing organizations focusing on teamwork and leadership, there are people speaking about intuition to male managers and leaders.

Carol: Linking intuition and profitability is now coming into mainstream corporate America. Fortunately, intuition is a word whose time has come.

John: I'm getting the sense from you, Carol, that listening is a tool for success. The success literature talks about changing beliefs—establishing positive and empowering beliefs. Still, I find it difficult to do. I'm sure I'm not alone out there. But listening is something I can get a handle on. I can deal with my listening.

Carol: When you start to deal with your listening, it's like catching your thoughts. You can *catch* a thought. You can hold a thought. We even say, "Hold that thought." You can train yourself to listen to things in a certain way. You can adapt to social trends and the idiosyncrasies of the era. We listen for trends, for the direction we're moving in, and adjust our thinking. Rules and regulations are general thoughts that we all subscribe to. They are really no more than that.

Holding a thought and creating a thought are the same thing. You can create a listening. You can hold a listening. A listening is something you can grab on to. It takes time in the beginning. After a while it becomes very simple.

John: Beyond individual listening there seems to be a collective listening that occurs—such as the "listening of the 1990s." With the 1980s it was, "Greed is good." The 1970s was the "me" decade.

Carol: Every decade has a listening.

John: So nations and cultures and corporations and teams and socioeconomic groups all have listenings?

Carol: Yes. It's important for us to recognize those as listenings because listenings can be changed. When I have an opinion about someone or something, there's actually a stop in energy. When I listen to someone, there's an opening. The word itself brings with it an openness. Opinions tend to be counter to each other. They tend to be antagonistic, unless they're in total agreement.

John: So that's where agree/disagree comes in. With opinions, the game that's being played is agree/disagree.

Carol: You can change your listening just like a radio station. You can prefer certain kinds of ways to listen to people. There's an energy exchange when you listen to people a certain way. If you listen to them from a strict opinion, then you have locked them in. One typical way we listen to people is to interrupt them. We finish people's sentences. We chime in like we already know what they're going to say. That immediately stifles the communication.

John: Why are we doing that?

Carol: There are many reasons: to demonstrate how smart we are or to convey something about ourselves: "I'm really here to please you" or "I'm really here to challenge you." It's about me, me, me, when I do that. Any time I interrupt, finish, or "add on to" without permission, without waiting for the other person, it's very me-oriented. We're not listening to anyone but ourselves.

John: In conversation, I often find myself becoming impatient with people. What's that about?

Carol: It could be a number of things, John. It could be that you're impatient for them to hurry up and finish what they have to say because what you have to say is far more valuable. You many have the thought that this person isn't listening to you and you want to get out of there. You may be impatient because they are interrupting you and cutting you off, or interrupting themselves and cutting themselves off. Some people don't even listen to what they themselves have to say, so the flow in their communication is choppy and disjointed. They're not complete because they're not listening and they're rushing through, anticipating that you're going to stop them because the rest of the world has interrupted them all their lives.

You need to pay close attention to how you communicate. How do you speak? And, more importantly, how do you listen?

Just recently I was working with some people and one of the individuals in the group was rushing to finish what he had to say. I recall saying, "Slow down. We are here to listen." His response was very revealing; he said, "I've always been told to hurry up because if I didn't, I would not be able to finish because somebody would finish for me." Can you imagine growing up as a child being told, "We're not going to listen to you long enough for you to finish what you have to say; we're going to finish it for you"?

John: When you become aware that you've become impatient, what do you do with that?

Carol: One thing you can do is to let people know. Say, "Sorry, I was thinking about something else. I'm back. Would you say that again?" Most people would think, "Oh, I can't do that—I can't tell somebody I checked out on them." The truth is, we check out on people all the time. We rarely hang around for a full conversation. We are busy thinking something else or judging, evaluating, waiting for someone to finish so we can finish whatever is going on with us at that moment. To tell someone brings us back to the present again. It lets the person know we really *are* interested—interested enough to let them know that we wandered away and then came back. That's how you start to train yourself—by catching yourself. Eventually you will act in your own best interest. If you keep drifting off and confessing enough, you're going to stop drifting quite so much.

John: In the midst of a conversation, I could say to the other person, "Pardon me, I was getting very impatient with the conversation and wasn't listening there for a bit; can you back up a little?" Is that what you're suggesting?

Carol: That is what I'm suggesting.

John: I can imagine that would shock people.

Carol: Yes, it could. While it may shock them, they become more attuned to speaking to you because they know now that they have your attention. They know when they lost it. We haven't been trained to say, "Are you still with me? Are you still listening?"

John: Carol, I want to talk more about children and the listening that is created as children. You spoke earlier about the "no's"—the reprimands most of us received as children. I remember this study where university students followed pre-school children around, counting the number of no's, negatives, stops, don't do this, and similar input they received during the day and the amount of positives—yes, oh, that is great—input they got. They counted something like

24

244 no's to 17 yes's. So I can understand how we have a listening that is molded by that. Say more, please, about what other listenings are established in childhood.

Carol: We make early childhood decisions that color our listening. For example, a woman told me that when she was three years old, her father bought her a turtle for her birthday. She took the turtle out of the little box it came in and, as turtles do, it started crawling around. Her father went out the front door to retrieve a newspaper, came back in, and stepped on the turtle. She was devastated, and she decided that she wasn't good because she'd allowed that to happen to the turtle. From that experience she became an adult overachiever to prove that she was good. But nothing was ever really finished or good enough for her after that incident. She always had to do one more thing—all out of that early decision. She kept looking for instances where she really wasn't good—if she didn't please Mommy or Daddy or the teachers.

As children, we make those kinds of decisions about ourselves. This affects our listening. Then we pick people to be around who will reinforce those childhood decisions and keep them in place. The schools we go to, the friends we have, the people we marry, the jobs we take on will reinforce those decisions.

When you can get back to the original source of what you thought as a little child, you can restructure your whole way of being out of a new listening for yourself. People can do that. I've seen it over and over again.

John: When we were talking about relationships, you mentioned the person who came home thirty minutes late and all the listening that was established around that. Are you saying that this happens to all of us in childhood? Are you saying that this is a universal phenomenon?

Carol: Yes. The phenomena that happen in childhood are often too much for us to handle as little people. We don't have enough life experiences to reach a logical conclusion about what happened. The little girl didn't know that turtles can get stepped on by big people who don't see them. At three years old, you don't think like that. What she saw was that she didn't take care of the turtle, which made her bad. When people go into therapy or counseling, it is not uncommon for them to remember certain things they did when they were little, things that resulted in behavior that continued all the way up to the current passion. If, as an adult, you can really recover that early thought you had, you can change it. You can change that listening. You made it up, and that is the liberating part of it. At the moment you discover what your listening was, you really have shifted and liberated forward motion.

John: You're saying that there are billions of people walking around on this planet in essence being controlled by the early decision of a three-year-old, a six-year-old.

Carol: That is what I'm saying. We have the thoughts of little children running our lives.

John: Okay. So how would I know, at the age of forty-nine, what these thoughts were? How would I get back to them?

Carol: Start looking at consistent patterns in your life. Start looking at the things that you repeat over and over—particularly the ones that are automatic. You may even announce your pattern—"Oh, here I go again." Start paying attention to those patterns. What are they? For example, suppose somebody says, "John, you talk too much," and you immediately think they don't like you. You can look at *why* you think they don't like you when they say you talk too much. Somewhere early on, you probably decided there was a link between talking and being liked. You become your own sleuth—"Where did this come from?" You have the information within you. You can start tracing it back by paying attention. Just take one thing at a time. If somebody says you talk too much, do you get indignant or irritated? What do you get out of someone telling you that you talk too much? Start to pay attention to that. Your reaction could indicate a pattern. Start to see where that pattern comes from.

John: I've certainly been accused of talking too much in the past, but that doesn't particularly resonate as something that's running me. Are you willing to help me look and see what might be?

Carol: Yes, I am.

Two
John Examines His Own Conditioning

John: So where do we begin?

Carol: Well, John, what comments typically irritate you?

John: There are so many things. . . . I hate it when people are stupid—in my judgment, of course. And I certainly am guilty of impatience.

Carol: What about opinions that don't agree with yours?

John: I've often thought that I live my life by being right. What that brings up is that I have a fear of confrontation. Even in conversation, I don't like to confront others. I don't do it very well. I don't confront my kids about behavior that doesn't work. That fear also comes up a whole lot with my wife Susan. I have trouble telling the truth about what I'm thinking and what I want. I'm afraid that I'm going to get rejected, that somebody won't like me. So in order to be liked, I'll do or say the convenient thing. Is there a clue in there?

Carol: You will do the "convenient thing." Is it to be liked or not to be tricked?

John: I've never thought about not being tricked. Bang! What that brings up right away is that I don't trust people.

Carol: You don't trust people. Let's take that one. What happened as a little kid that made you not trust people? What did people do to you? What happened?

John: Being falsely accused drove me crazy. I remember an incident from elementary school. I was afraid some older kids would beat me up if I told the truth about the incident and said what really happened. They caused a commotion in a school assembly and blamed me for something I didn't do. The teacher yanked me out of the assembly and didn't believe that I was telling the truth. I was afraid. That kind of thing happened to me four or five times. And I've thought about this for years, this false accusation stuff.

Based upon what we have been talking about, I can see that I think that older people, authority figures—people like that—can't be trusted. If I tell the truth, I still won't be trusted. These people are not to be trusted with my life, the events of my life. So there is that fear.

Carol: Good. Now take that fear. You said something about being beaten up. You were afraid these authority figures were going to do something to harm you, so you couldn't trust them. This is around age eleven. Now go back even earlier—somewhere around age three or four?

John: Hum . . . something happened at three or four? Well, it had nothing to do with being beat up, I don't think. I was born with something called native conjunctivitis. I glibly refer to it as my "birth defect." The common name for it is blocked tear ducts. The blocked tear ducts would cause this discharge to come out the corners of my eyes. When I was four years old, my mom and another relative took me to a Park Avenue specialist in New York who suggested that I have an operation. So I was put into a hospital. The plan was to drill holes in the bridge of my nose to open up these tear

29

ducts because bone was blocking the ducts. I've since learned that this condition can be thoroughly controlled with diet—that it didn't have anything to do with bone, but medical knowledge has advanced a lot in forty-five years.

I remember going into this high-ceilinged hospital that looked like the old insane asylums of the 1860s, with leaded glass windows that looked sixty feet high. The image that comes to mind is sitting in the end of a ward with other children and their parents. My mom was there. She had gotten me a hook-and-ladder fire truck, which was very expensive in those days. I had wanted one for a long time, and I had to get my butt into a hospital in order to get this fire truck.

As I'm telling this story I can see how I was developing thoughts about how to live life successfully.

I remember not being scared or crying, but being very disoriented. Eventually my mother left the hospital. This was the first time in my life I'd been separated from my mom.

It was pretty traumatic. I remember crying and missing her and being scared because it was dark and strange. I know I went to sleep because my memory is that I was physically shaken awake. It was pitch black. I'd guess it was 4:30 or 5:00 in the morning. I was lifted out of my crib and put on a gurney. I remember being groggy and then becoming conscious and being really scared because the nurses had masks on. So here I am being yanked out of my crib in the early morning hours and my mom is nowhere around. I don't recall doing this, but my imagination says I probably was crying, "Mommy, Mommy," not knowing what the heck was going on.

I started to panic and kick my legs. I remember flailing back and forth. I remember them strapping me down. I got totally strapped down—straps across my knees, across my chest and my arms. But my memory is of *being imprisoned.*

This is interesting because it's only been in the last five years or so that I've ceased to be claustrophobic. It's amazing how these images are coming back. I remember being whisked down the hall, lying on my back, looking at the lights flying by overhead. Eventually, I'm just freaking out, totally hysterical.

I end up in an operating room. Everything is dark except for this huge light, which is like the sun over my head. I'm still freaking out. From the shadows emerges this masked woman. She's trying to get me to calm down. She says she'll show me a Mickey Mouse movie if I'll be quiet. Well, I didn't care for Mickey Mouse. I didn't have a good listening for Mickey Mouse at that point in time. Then she asks me if I like Donald Duck.

Now she's got me because I loved Donald Duck. I remember getting it together a little bit and saying yes, I like Donald Duck. She said, "If I show you a Donald Duck movie, will you calm down, stop crying?" I'm sure my response came between sobs, trying to sniffle back tears. I remember that the moment I calmed down, this woman takes this floppy, rubber, yellow, oaken color facemask and places it over my mouth and nose. Everything went black. It was like I died.

Carol: Yes. You died.

John: I guess the ultimate "beat-up" is being beaten to death.

Carol: Yes. Being beaten to death, and you were tricked. Lied to.

John: Yes. And tricked by someone in authority, by a woman. And the whole conspiracy set up by Mother who was the only one I could trust. Oh, this is rich, Carol.

Carol: Yes.

John: It seems like a little more than having my turtle stepped on.

Carol: That depends on the three- or four-year-old. Anyway, therein is the beginning of your pattern, John. You don't trust adults, especially adults in authority, because they may be manipulative. You may get tricked. And here is the kicker, John: look and see if it's women in authority who may trick you.

John: Do I have to look and see? Am I sitting here with you today thinking you are going to trick me?

Carol: That may not be a conscious thought, but it could be somewhere lurking in the back as a reaction to your environment. That thought is not too far away; it's lingering. Even if I couldn't deliberately trick you, there may be something that might get tricky about what we are doing today. I may pull a fast one, do something unexpected.

John: And do I have, unbeknownst to me, a listening for that?

Carol: Yes.

John: I have a distrust of politicians. I have a distrust of the police. I've worked for myself for years because I don't want a boss. Is this all a product of this listening that I developed with a decision as a four-year-old?

Carol: Yes it is, John. And there are many factors that came in to give you further evidence. That was the beginning. That was *a number one* trauma for you as a child. After that first incident, you've looked for additional evidence to validate that what you made up in that moment was true.

John: Then being falsely accused in school "plugged me in"—reactivated that earlier trauma.

I remember at age fourteen or fifteen watching a football game on TV with my dad on Sunday afternoon. He was always after me to participate and contribute, to be considerate. I remember picking myself off the couch during the game and saying to myself, *you know what, I'm going to do a good thing, I'm going to be considerate, I'm going to sweep the porch.* I remember going to the closet in the kitchen where the broom and the dustpan were kept. I remember opening the front door with the broom in one hand and the dustpan in the other and hearing my dad call from the living room, "Why don't you do something useful like sweep the porch?" I was livid! I felt so furious and so ripped off. I was on my way to do that very thing, but I knew he would never believe me. Here is another authority figure whom I can't trust.

Carol: Yes.

John: Seems like all of those incidents, or evidence, contribute to some other decision besides "I can't trust them." "I can't trust them" is about *them.* What about *me*?

Carol: You are helpless. Were you not helpless at that moment that mask was put over your face?

John: Yes.

Carol: You say, "They're not going to believe me anyway." You may not say it out loud, but you think that. What you're saying is, "I'm helpless in this situation. No matter what I say, nobody is going to believe me." You're helpless. And, John, you go 180 degrees the other way.

John: I was about to say I'm now the least helpless person I know.

Carol: Absolutely. You will work yourself until you're burned out to demonstrate that you are anything but helpless.

John: "I'll show you. I can do this."

Carol: You bet. And you work at being "better than" others so that you will never be perceived as helpless—running from a decision that you made when you couldn't do anything about that mask being put over your face.

John: Okay. This is a little much here. Are you telling me that the motivation to sell over a million copies of books, to become financially successful, to have a gorgeous house, are all driven by my doing anything I can do to prove that I'm not helpless? Are you saying that this decision I made as a four-year-old is running my life?

Carol: Yes.

John: And that is all my listening.

Carol: Yes, it's all your listening. Something you listened to as a little one. And I really appreciate your using the word "driven" because you are not making a choice about it. You *are* driven. You are not inspired. You are not moving from your vision or being passionate about something. You are being *driven*. And underlying this is the thought that you might be helpless, you might not be able to pull this off—like when you were four years old.

John: And I will do anything to avoid that.

Carol: Yes, you will.

John: So if I'm in a conversation with Susan and it isn't working and I feel helpless to change it, I get out of there as fast as possible.

Carol: Yes, you get out of there or you have the other person exit.

John: Or raise my voice or use my intelligence to defeat her so that the *threat* goes away.

Carol: Absolutely.

John: At forty-nine years old, I'm doing this, being run by a life-long listening of a decision made as a four-year-old. And I'm not the only one on the planet living like this, right?

Carol: That is correct. Everybody is doing this. Now, there's good news too.

John: Oh, please say more about that.

Carol: The good news is that once you get what you just walked yourself through, you can see you are *now* an adult. You have children of your own, John, so you know how frightened four-year-old children can be. Now you can have compassion for this four-year-old John who is still within you. You understand that this child made some very strong decisions about something that happened long ago, with very little information. You can have compassion for that and also say that's not true *now*. When you find yourself reacting to something, you can look at it and say, "What is the threat here? What am I listening to that has me threatened?"

John: Is that the question that I ask in the moment? Can you restate that question?

Carol: What is the threat here? What am I afraid of in this moment/ What is it that's happening in this conversation? It's a "what" question, not a "why" question, and it's important to understand the distinction between *why* and *what*. When you say "Why am I . . . ?" that simply keeps you on the treadmill of more answers and more answers and more answers, which doesn't get to what. What happened? What is it that's going on with me right now? "What" puts you in the present. "Why" keeps you removed.

John: I'm not clear about that.

Carol: We have to come to the present to look at what just happened. If we ask the question, "Why am I like this?" we are now removed from the present; we're off somewhere else, generally looking at the past. We are not present to what is right in front of us. "Is this truly a threat right now?" takes you out of that old past behavior. So you just state what is happening now. Am I being threatened right now? Am I really being threatened by Susan at this time? What has she said that has threatened me? What am I reacting to? Do I really think she's going to trick me?"

36

John: When I think of conversations where I've been argumentative or yelled or left, I was certainly guilty of speaking before I thought. They were emotionally-charged situations. So I have to slow things down to get access to that "What is threatening here?" question.

Carol: Yes, and one way is to stop in that moment and say to yourself, "Wait a minute, I'm reacting here. Wait. Just a minute." You don't even have to go all the way back to being four years old. You can say, "Wait, Susan, what just happened here? First we were talking about this and now 'boom' I'm off and upset with you. What happened?"

You've got a person who loves you sitting across from you. You're having a conversation and all of a sudden you're acting like there's this imminent threat; and there isn't! As a little child, you made up certain things about people. If anybody shows up with a mask, you get suspicious.

John: And there's a biological manifestation of that. I can't breathe. Rather than having to deal with something as insurmountable as a phobia, I can shift my listening. I can do this through something as simple as changing my listening. That's a lot less challenging—even though it's obviously hard work.

Carol: Yes.

John: I've been married for seventeen years. I'm sure that Susan would love to have a hundred dollars for every time I've been threatened and felt helpless in a conversation and responded negatively or argumentatively to her.

Carol: Those are all cues for you. Any time you respond

negatively, harshly, with criticism, you have somehow felt threatened. Otherwise, why is there a need for you to respond that way? There's something you're listening to.

John: Just so I know this isn't all about me, is everybody doing this? I mean, you do too?

Carol: Absolutely.

John: I have thoughts and judgments about people who are helpless, which is how I'm afraid I am. Is that my deepest, darkest fear coming up? What kind of person is helpless? If I find helpless, needy people, I have no use for them.

Carol: Like helpless people are useless?

John: Yes.

Carol: They just shouldn't even be around?

John: I know we disparaged logic just a little earlier, but logically where I go with that is that if I'm helpless, then people won't have a use for me.

If we have an entire world of adults who are walking around with fears that their childhood decision is who they are, who are driven to be anything but that, then we live in a world of creatures based on pretense.

Carol: That's accurate. We all have our facade, our pretense. We all have our personality that we have developed to hide something. Haven't you heard people say, "If they really knew me, they might not like me?"

John: Sure.

Carol: Well, that's another form of saying, "They'll find out about my decision." The other thing, John, is that it's not all that obvious. People don't know that they've made that kind of a decision. They have no idea.

John: No, clearly I did not walk into this conversation with you realizing that I felt helpless and useless and the extent to which that runs my life by the way I listen to myself. Is listening like expectation? In other words, if I have a certain listening, do I have an expectation?

Carol: Absolutely. And it's an *automatic* listening. It's an automatic, reactive, lazy listening, which creates the expectation. By the same token, you can create an "empowered listening," which brings with it a *different* expectation. You see, expectations work both ways. If you have a *disempowering* listening about yourself, then you create self-limitation. If you have a listening that "I can do anything; there isn't anything in this world I can't do," you will raise yourself to that kind of accomplishment. That's an expectation. You expect yourself to be a brilliant writer, so you are. That's because that's you're listening. "I can accomplish anything. I am a competent speaker. I am an excellent technician. I am a wealthy human being. I am a rich person with friends. I am kind. I am generous. I am a good friend."

When you *listen* to those things about yourself, you *are* those things; you live up to those expectations.

John: It seems to me that most of the listening out there is not "I am a wealthy individual" but rather "I am poor." It's the negative listening that predominates.

Carol: Yes, it does. As you mentioned earlier, by the time we're five or six, we have heard at least 244 you can'ts, don'ts, shouldn'ts, to just a few you can's. So that's what predominates. We carry forward the negative things that we hear as children. By the time you were in the operating room as a child, you already had enough of that. When they put that yellow mask over your face, you felt helpless. It all reinforced what had already been on its way. That's true for all of us. Now, the phenomenon of listening restores that to us. People hear *us*; they don't hear the *negativity*. That's why it's important to listen to people unconditionally, without your agenda.

John: So the listening that you're proposing immediately cuts through all of this programmed pattern we've created. That wide-open listening that you spoke about doesn't acknowledge this made-up stuff because it's listening for something else. Is that true?

Carol: It's not "listening for something else." As a person listens to you, they hear the totality of you, not the selective things that you have brought with you—all that negative self-talk that's going on. When you listen to someone, truly listen, you listen to the entirety of the person's communication. And the totality of their communication releases them from the negative frame of reference. You're not reinforcing it. You reinforce it when you're busy thinking about something else.

John: And if I'm listening to me as "I am capable," there's not much room in there for "I'm helpless and useless."

Carol: In empowered listening there is another very, very powerful state that I want to talk about. I call it the "Zen of listening." It means that I really transcend; I become disciplined. It's a self-discipline. You transcend and the other person is able to transcend any of their negative self-talk. It becomes almost a meditative state, John. And you become interconnected with that other person, with their energy and their communication. You begin to walk in their shoes as they speak. It's an amazing phenomenon. It's like our two energies—our two systems—combine. We don't lose ourselves in each other, however. We both become larger, both of us at the same time. That's the Zen of listening.

Three

The Zen of Listening

John: I'm not sure that I understand Zen. What does that mean?

Carol: Zen teaches self-discipline, deep meditation and an attainment of enlightenment. That's how I understand Zen. You use intuition and you get insight and you start to self-validate what you know to be so. It goes beyond intellectual conception or logic. When you have the Zen listening, you stop thinking; you become more present to what's immediately in front of you. You start to experience the energy between you and the other person. You start to really hear the words that are being spoken. All of a sudden, you have an expanded awareness. It isn't anything you can figure out. This is not something you can logically do. It becomes a self-discipline, a practice. Which is why it's hard work in the beginning. You're taking on a discipline, a way of training yourself, that eventually will have people be complete and whole around you.

Now, when I start to talk about that, people say, yeah, well, that sounds kind of woo-woo and New Age. Fortunately, it isn't woo-woo. And it isn't New Age either. It is something that the quantum physicists are now talking about. We have an electromagnetic field that scientists are able to measure. They're beginning to determine what happens when people are really in communication with each other. Our energy fields change. The Zen of listening means that you "become one" with that other person's energy; the two energies merge without losing either of us. We are both intact, and we have an energy exchange.

How does that work in business? How does that work with relationships? It works immeasurably well. When you stop talking and start listening to someone's desires, someone's needs, their ability to accomplish something, you've actually supported them in carrying out their mission. You may have sat and just listened to someone, and they say, "Wow, John, thank you. Boy, we sure had a great conversation." And you haven't said much at all. You *listened*. And what they've received is the validation. They've returned to who they really are, their true self. You have entered into that partnership with them at a very deep level. It's almost a meditative level. People don't start out there. However, once you start working with listening that's what eventually happens.

John: You brought to mind a story that a friend of ours, Richard Brooke, has told many times about a scientific experiment by a psychiatrist who was flying First Class from New York to Los Angeles. The task for the psychiatrist was to engage his seat mate in a conversation. But the psychiatrist would offer no information, would give no declarative statements, wouldn't say a thing about himself. All he would do was ask questions. The flight lasted six hours. A research team met the plane as it landed in Los Angeles and conducted an interview with this psychiatrist's seat mate.

Two things came out of that research that I find fascinating. One was that the psychiatrist's seat mate—and remember the psychiatrist did nothing but ask this person questions—said that the psychiatrist was the single most fascinating person he had ever met in his life. And the second piece of information was that he didn't know the psychiatrist's name.

That seems to corroborate exactly what you spoke about. It sounds like by listening, you can show up at your best.

Carol: Yes.

John: This seems to be the Zen of listening. One manifestation of Zen is this incredibly uncluttered, undistracted, being present in the moment—like there's nothing else for me now but being in this room with you—no thought, no "this means that." It's just "be here now."

Carol: If there is an ultimate in listening, that's it—the Zen of listening, to "be here now." You notice we're never any place else but here. Except our thoughts are often not here. Our listening is not here. Our listening is often anywhere else but here. Our listening is with our checkbook. Our listening is what we did last year, or ten years ago, or what we will be doing twenty years from now.

John: Carol, the moment I hear that, I'm back in that event that happened when I was four, the decisions that I made. Did something similar to that happen for you in your life? Can you tell me your story?

Carol's Story

Carol: Oh, yes. My mother worked for the United States Government in what was called a stenographer's pool, so she had to take me to a babysitter. Miss Tina. And because my mother worked, she was able to give me almost everything I needed and a goodly number of things I wanted. For breakfast I had oatmeal and apples and toast and milk and juice. I went to Miss Tina's with a full tummy every morning. I also had a little lunch that my mother would pack for me.

Miss Tina took care of other children as well. Their parents, for whatever reasons, didn't supply them with lunch, so she would have a makeshift breakfast—toast and some milk and little slices of cheddar cheese. At noon, she would take *my* lunch and divide it up among the other children. I would get really, really angry with her for doing that. I was very little and Miss Tina was a very short, very broad woman; the most I could see was the lower part of her rear end, most of the time. I remember one afternoon when she took my lunch as usual. It must have been a "bad hair day" for me because I went up and bit her in the rear end. Just took a big chunk out of her rear end.

John: Oh, no!

Carol: Oh, yes. I was still wearing diapers, and I remember she picked me up, turned me over, pulled down my diaper and bit me back.

John: Wow!

Carol: At that point, I decided, one, that you really couldn't trust people because they would bite you. And, two, if you spoke out or responded in action, you would get hurt. So I figured that I could never be *enough* after that. Everybody around me was bigger than I was. So, in that moment, I decided I wasn't *enough*. I wasn't *enough* to bite her back. There wasn't *enough* of my lunch to go around. There just wasn't *enough*.

For years, John, my whole life was about having excess. I would buy two and three and four of everything as far

45

back as I can remember. I have bought excesses of everything. My closets used to look like a warehouse because I didn't want to run out of toilet paper, napkins, straws, those paper bathroom cups. I always had too much. So stuff would spoil in my house. I didn't have any idea that this childhood decision was what I was driven by. I just thought you were supposed to have plenty so that you never run out. I would sometimes run out of money because I would buy more stuff than I needed.

I started to do this work, this exploration of what makes Carol McCall tick. In one instance, I had an opportunity to regress back to the time of my birth. I actually had a chance to go back to the early thoughts about being born. I knew that my mother had problems delivering me. She had arthritis, so the bones in her cervical area didn't open enough for me to pass through the birth canal; she would only dilate so far. They finally had to come in and pull me out with forceps. Somehow under this hypnosis I remembered thinking that I can't do this. I am not "enough." I am not "enough" because I couldn't come through the birth canal.

I have since checked it out with therapists and people who are very, very familiar with where we really begin to develop our personalities and the way we think. I was able to see that in the birth canal, I had decided I wasn't enough. Then, when this incident happened with Miss Tina, that was another traumatic moment for me. That solidified it. From that point on, everything that happened indicated that I wasn't enough.

I remember trying to meet my mother after her work one day. I must have been five or six. I was standing on the corner, waiting for her bus to come. It felt like I waited there all night, although actually it was just a couple of hours. It turned out I was at the wrong bus stop. I thought my mother wouldn't come home because I wasn't enough to bring her

46

home. *And Mama is working because I am not enough. I can't do enough for Mama. What can I do for her?* That has driven me up until the last fifteen years. It took me that long to get in touch with this driving energy that I had about making sure that I had plenty of everything, that I was enough. I always over-achieved with grades. I overachieved in my relationships with people. I was accused of being too intense.

I always took on more. When I was first married, I went back to school to get my master's degree. I was also in practice to be a therapist and running for the Community College School Board. And I was applying to run George McGovern's political campaign. I took on all manner of things to prove that I was enough.

Now I make choices about the things that I take on. I've discovered that I have the ability to handle a number of things because I got healed from having been driven. So now I make choices about them. I look and see all the different projects I choose to take on, not what I'm *driven* to take on.

John: When I look at these childhood decisions you've talked about, I see mostly the negatives. From what you just said, I wonder: Are these decisions also useful? Can we use them to create success in empowering ways?

Carol: Yes, you can. The turning point for me, fifteen years ago, was to really get clear that in being driven to do all of that, the listening that I had was that I wasn't enough. I remember one day receiving an acknowledgment of something that I had done from someone I respected. It was, "Carol McCall, you really are a handful." Well "a handful" to me meant enough, a lot, a sufficient amount. I had never, ever thought of myself as "a handful." There was a shift deep within me. I got it. "Wow, I do a lot!"

It is really to my advantage when I'm not driven to prove anything. I know how to do lots of different things at the same time. I have an internal system in place that will have me be successful with things I take on concurrently. And that isn't so bad. What *isn't* healthy is when I am doing this to prove something—when I go unconscious, lose my awareness, go back to an automatic non-thinking reactive way of listening to myself.

John: What was the age when this butt-biting incident occurred?

Carol: I was three years old.

John: My early childhood decision was made at age four. You had an event that occurred at age three. I remember your saying earlier that somewhere between one and five we have one of these.

Four

How We Learn to Cope

Carol: Everybody has something like this that happened to them during their childhood, generally in the first five years. Then it gets updated. The early decisions we make get solidified from ages six through twelve.

John: Is that like a refinement?

Carol: Yes. For example, if something happens for a one-year-old and they don't know quite how to handle it, they will dismiss it. They won't deal with it because they don't know how. What does a one-year-old know how to do? A traumatic experience could be something as simple as crying in their crib and nobody comes to them. That child will either dismiss that situation, because it is too painful, or they will decide that people dismiss them. Out of deciding that, they will start to dismiss others. You'll see people who shrug stuff off and say, "Well, whatever," or "So what?" That's an indication of dismissal. Language will let you know, generally, where people are. That is an example of what might happen for someone one year old.

John: Does each age have a different type of thing happen?

Carol: Yes.

John: Would it be reasonable to say that inside all of us, as adults, is a one-year-old or a two-year-old or a three-year-old, depending on when this pivotal event occurred for us?

Carol: I would say so. Our listening gets influenced by our natural human development. At every stage of our growth, something gets left out that, if it were put in, would have us be healthy, fully-functioning human beings without filters. Somewhere in our growth, something didn't happen. We didn't get attention. We had to move and leave friends. Growing up as human beings, things do happen to us. And we don't know how to take care of these as growing, developing little people. How do we take care of another human being? There are no manuals. We see certain practices passed on and, in this passing, healthy things get missed.

The major thing that happens, John, is that children don't get heard. They don't get listened to. This is an ongoing pattern all the way up to age twelve. Well, if you don't get listened to at age one, you might determine that you should be dismissed. You are not important. Then if you don't get listened to at age two, which is an age of exploration for children, you might determine you can't explore, you can't reach out. You can't go here, or you can't go there.

Around two we start to say "no" to authority because we are testing out our own power. If we get thwarted by not being listened to, one of the things we will do is push against our parent or the authority. We will also get very suspicious. "What are you up to? What are you trying to keep me from doing?" That's something that a little two-year-old might do. Then if we are not listened to again at three, we might think "Here we go again. They've been doing this to me since I got here." As a three-year-old, we want so badly to show that we know something; we begin to use the term "I know." Or "Let me tell. Or "Let me show you." This is especially true if there are younger siblings around.

Age three is a show-and-tell time. These children will point and say, "You people did this" or "You people did that" or "I know about those people." They are still going through their developmental stages. At the age of four, they are beginning to do another version of what they did at two. They are beginning to get a little more sophisticated. At two we say, "What are you up to?" as if suspicious. At four we say, "People won't let me."

John: And that's what I got into?

Carol: Yes. You did what you needed to do.

Now we are moving into age five, and still people are not listening. So what do we have left as children? We start to strike out: "I will beat you. I will play this game and I will beat you." Five-year-olds are wise children, and they begin to listen to the world to see how they can win and not lose. It is very much about winning. In fact, it's "I win, you lose. I'm right, you're wrong."

Also at the age of five, there is: "You don't understand." There is that testing again, an updated version of what you do at two. "Are you conning me? Are you trying to make me stupid?" These little decisions are coming into play and the child is adding to this as he or she is growing.

At age six: "Who do you think you are?" "Why does this always happen to me?" "Don't make quick decisions." This is very similar to the dismissive "whatever." Each time it repeats itself, it's upgraded. By the time you're twelve, it's "Do it my way or hit the highway," another version of "You're wrong and I'm right."

If you don't know that you have these filters because something was missing as you were raised, you're going to bring all of them with you as you develop. By the time you're twelve or thirteen, you say and think all of these. "Let me show you." "Show me, prove it." And you can hear yourself as an adult saying it. You'll begin to be attracted to

people who reinforce those early decisions. So if you don't
trust people, you're going to tend to hang out with others
who don't trust people. We reinforce our early decisions. It
would be uncomfortable for you to hang out with people
who trusted people. You would probably find them very
gullible, very vulnerable, not safe. You might end up getting
tricked. But with people who don't trust, you're going to
feel a kinship, because you are listening to the world the
same way, like it is not safe here.

The human being is always working through a process
called "physis," which means a natural evolution towards
health. We are always moving to get healthy. Yet we live in
an environment that doesn't always allow us to be healthy.
We don't get certain things we need. In psychological terms,
these are called "lacunae"—like holes in our personality. By
listening and being heard, you can begin to fill in these
holes. Listening heals those areas that got missed when you
were little.

Suppose you surrounded yourself with people who listen—a listening community—let's say for the next ninety
days. Suppose all the people did was listen to you. In ninety
days many of the areas that were unfulfilled for you as a
child could get fulfilled. You would begin to move forward
very quickly and powerfully. You'd begin to hear things differently, to see things differently. You would even begin to
speak differently because you were heard. That dynamic
process would allow you to complete those areas that you
didn't complete as a youngster.

John: And you're saying we all go through each and every
phase. But there is one predominant one, and that is the one
based on not being heard. Can you say more about that?

Carol: The predominant one comes in the most traumatic

part of your life. For you, John, that was the hospital event. For me, the one that I recalled most predominantly was the butt-biting event.

John: Or for the little girl, it was the turtle that was stepped on.

Carol: Yes, exactly. Now, after that you will find other incidents that will reinforce that most traumatic one. You will act as though each one is the same as what happened to you the first time.

John: So now I'm forming a pattern, like a habit.

Carol: Yes. And nobody heard the pain. Nobody heard you. Nobody listened to what you had to say. I remember when I told my mother that Miss Tina had bitten me. She asked me, "Well, what did you do, Carol Ann? Did you bite Miss Tina?" I said "Yes, I did, but she took my lunch and she was giving it to everybody else."

My mother didn't hear me. She said, "You were not a good little girl. Miss Tina had to make you an example." I was upset. I wondered, *how could you say that? How could you not support me and come to my rescue. I'm a little girl, she's taking my stuff, and you are supporting her.* Again, I felt not enough. Now at that time, I didn't know that's what I felt, but I knew I felt devastated that I couldn't get my mother to understand.

John: Is there something like betrayal in there?

Carol: Absolutely. People will betray you. They will bite you in the behind. So watch out. Cover your back.

John, to this day, I will sit in a restaurant with my back

to the wall. Now I can laugh at it because I know what it is and yet I will look for a seat in a restaurant with my back to the wall because I don't want anybody biting me in the behind.

John: You know, I don't go to hospitals. I actually thought it was a religious decision because my mother was a Christian Scientist. It's hard to think of it being because I made a decision based on an event when I was a four-year-old.

So there is a world full of one, two, five, six, and twelve-year-olds running big corporations and countries and having wars.

Carol: Yes. I had the opportunity to sit in at the Fiftieth Anniversary celebration of the United Nations a few years ago. I had a chance to listen to the world's heads of state, a true privilege. And immediately I was struck by, wait a minute, wait a minute. They are not listening. Russia is not listening to China. Mexico is not listening to Italy. Rumania is not listening to France. It became clear to me that we don't listen—no matter what country we live in. We really don't listen. I think, John, that when people start to master listening, really master listening, we won't have any more wars. We won't have any need for that.

John: If enough of us, whatever that number needs to be, begin to listen as you are encouraging us to do, what else will change on this planet?

Carol: When enough of us listen, first of all, we won't have children who are abused. Therefore we will not have convicts who murder and kill people because they were abused and nobody heard them. We won't have poverty because people will hear that there is enough. We have a listening called scarcity and when you shift that listening to abundance, there will be enough to go around. John, there really is enough to go around. When people can listen to that, we become a community that begins to care for each other. We wouldn't allow people to go homeless.

Our educational system would certainly change. We would have children coming out with both hemispheres fully developed—right brain, left brain. We'd have more artists, creative geniuses, physicists and engineers who could take us to other planets, to other galaxies, because we listened. I see all kinds of possibilities. That is the kind of world I am interested in creating through listening. It may seem like such a dream, so farfetched. Well, putting a man on the moon seemed like a dream too. And we did that.

John: Is listening contagious? When people begin to develop the kind of listening that you're speaking about, does that have a tendency to multiply?

Carol: I think so, John. People who have started to really master this listening, and haven't gone back to their old habits or old patterns of listening, say they've noticed that people around them have started to listen. Mothers say that when they've started to listen, their children are listening in return. A husband said, "You know, I've started to listen to my wife and she's starting to listen to what I have to say." He had been offering her all kinds of advice and telling her how to do it and problem solving, and she had not been listening. The minute he started to listen to her, she started to listen to him. Yes, I think it is contagious.

I think it has a domino effect. As with that Hundredth Monkey story, when enough people start to do something, that action reaches a critical mass and everybody starts to do it. That's what I'm counting on with listening.

John: Let me ask you: If kids were really being listened to, would we be operating on these childhood decisions?

Carol: Because of how we're raised initially, I think childhood decisions would still occur, but they wouldn't be as detrimental to our growth because, out of being heard, we can get self-validated. You know the story you told about the psychiatrist who only asked questions of his seat mate on the plane? The seat mate got to hear about himself, so he got off that plane feeling very validated. The most fascinating person he had been talking to was really himself; it was like a mirroring. Children can be mirrored when they are listened to. That energy is given back to them. Their decisions can be quickly dissipated out of being heard—as long as we reduce the negative do's and don't that we give them as well. I think the two have to go hand in hand. When children are heard, they will self-correct. So we may not have to do as many do's and don'ts for them.

John: Carol, aren't a lot of those don'ts intended to keep children safe—to protect them? Isn't that the role of parents? As a parent, I don't want my child to go touching the hot stove or playing with matches. Where is the distinction between what seems like a very high-minded thing to do and that negativity that squishes kids' spirits or limits their development?

Carol: When you're raising children with do's and don'ts for their safety, you can also tell them that it's for their safety. That is very different from automatically telling them just don't because I said so. "Don't cross the street with the cars running because you could get hurt. I don't want you to get hurt." Of course, a child is not going to remember that. You can keep reminding the child, "Don't cross the street when the cars are coming; you will get hurt." That is different from "Don't do it because I said so" or "Don't be a bad girl." If I said to you, "John, don't put the glass of water too close to the end of the table; it will spill," that's very different from saying or implying, "Don't do that—you're irritating me."

John: Even if you say to me, "Don't put your glass there because it may get knocked over, make a mess, break the glass, and you'll be embarrassed"—all that positive stuff—I may have a one-through-twelve listening, and it's going to fall into some other category. Which has nothing to do with the positive directive you just gave me.

Carol: You are always going to have to work to keep that kind of listening at bay. It means being present, being here now. If I'm talking to you and you say, "Carol, say more about that," if I allow myself to get reactive or lazy in my listening, I could easily hear that as, *uh-oh, I am not enough.*

John: Even though I was actually interested to learn more?

Carol: Exactly. I am automatically thrown back into that old reactive pattern if I am not staying present—staying aware and conscious—to what you are saying and what I am saying. Because I am clear that there is interest on your face and I can tell from the way you're asking me that you want to hear more. Being present, I can pick that up. If I'm listening to those old tapes, listening to that old reactive decision that I made, I'm not going to hear your interest. I'm going to hear what I have already made up.

John: What is this trigger? It seems that because of the listening, this early childhood decision, there is tremendous opportunity to go off half-cocked, to get upset, angry, all kinds of melodrama based on these erroneous decisions.

Carol: It is like the trigger, as you said. It puts into motion a particular cycle that we have called a "drama cycle." If you could step back and look at it, it would be funny. Because *anything* can trigger you—a twitch of the eyebrow, someone clearing their throat, someone looking away from you for a moment to think. Anything can trigger you when you're upset, when you're tired, when you have incompletions in your life, in your day.

John: What do you mean, incompletions?

Carol: Things you haven't completed or finished or accomplished—for example, the letter you were supposed to write and didn't get out, or that phone call you didn't return. That's what I men by incompletions. They pile up by the end of the day and contribute to your going off half-cocked, as you put it. We walk around with a lot of incompletions, which can trigger the proverbial "final straw"—that word and/or gesture that will have us go into our drama cycle.

John: Why do we have these drama cycles? Suppose I have this sincere request: I say, "Carol, tell me more about that." Is that enough to trigger you? What would happen next?

Carol: I could go to "Oh, he thinks I'm not enough," and I would feel sad. Because of that sadness, I will speed up what I have to say, or get more articulate, get very intelligent, bring in lots of information about the subject, to prove I am enough.
    Then I continue on in my drama cycle. The next thing I

58

will do is have a thought: I wonder if I've done enough. Have I said enough? Did this do it? That thought will generate another feeling in me called fear or anxiety. When I'm anxious, I either talk faster or I slow down and get deliberate, really wanting to appear calm, like I have everything under control.

John: But you're boiling inside?

Carol: Yes, I am boiling inside. I'm acting like I've calmed down, but my thought is still, this isn't enough. I bet he knows I don't have any more to say. Now I start feeling very angry with you because you still are sitting there looking at me with this frown on your face, like you don't understand what I'm talking about. Because of the anger, I begin to get very short with my answers. I won't give you a full sentence. My words actually become clipped. I start to cut myself off. Then I also have a thought about that: Oh boy, I bet he thinks I'm being smart-alecky, trying to show off.

So where do I go with that thought? I start to feel embarrassed because I really don't want you to think that—and notice, now, you haven't said a word. You're sitting there just looking at me, listening to me. I'm going around this imaginary clock—this cycle of drama. My behavior becomes trying to please you because I certainly, definitely want to please you. So I will start to lean forward and look at you and smile and make sure I'm doing this thing right.

John: It's interesting—through this whole explanation, your face has changed nine or ten times. Different expressions. And you're not experiencing these things, you're just describing what happens.

59

Carol: I know how each of these things feels in my own drama cycle. There is a bodily sensation to it. Now, I'm almost at the end of this cycle. As I smile and lean forward, I'm thinking, *Okay, I think I've done enough here. I'm sure he's got the point by now.* So I'll start to shake my head and look to you for agreement because I'm supposed to be pleasing you and you're supposed to be picking that up.

If you are still sitting there scowling, I'm going to think, *Oh, this still wasn't enough. He still didn't get it.* I get really resigned, like *Well, what's the point? Why bother" He's never going to get this one.* I withdraw and I'm back at the top of my cycle called "it is not enough," which is exactly where I started when you said, "Tell me more about that, Carol."

I've now gone full circle, counterclockwise, all around my drama cycle. Every one of us has our drama cycle, which starts with a thought, followed by a feeling, followed by a behavior. It is the most amazing, fascinating behavior I have ever watched in people.

John: It doesn't sound like much fun.

Carol: Well, it isn't fun when you're *in* it. And, there is a way to get *out* of it. In that moment that it feels real, we simply need to speak what we are feeling in that moment. Let's say, for example, that I was in my drama cycle. I was thinking that you think I'm a show-off and I got embarrassed. I could say to you, "John, I'm embarrassed. I think you think I'm showing off." This stops the cycle just like that. Because then I would be present again to what is going on with me in that moment. I could get that you were listening, and that you wanted to know more. You weren't telling me I wasn't enough. I was the one who was off and running, telling myself that.

John: When you have the information you need, do you also get that you are enough?

Carol: Yes. When you were listening to me as I went around my drama cycle, I was very clear that I was not only enough, I was actually encouraged and inspired to go on, to really finish it. I was so excited because I was really getting that you were getting it. I was encouraged to move on, to go forward, to give you more of myself.

That's what listening does for people: it empowers them to give you more. When you can stop yourself in your drama cycle and the other person is present, you can see that the drama cycle has nothing to do with *them* and everything to do with *you*. Then you can be returned to yourself: "Oh, I see. I made this up."

I don't expect this to sound easy, as though you can listen to a tape, read a book, or try it once and you've got it. Breaking your drama cycle, learning how to listen to others, how to empower others is a daily, day-in-day-out discipline. You must put it into practice, into life, on a regular basis. Most people don't want to do that. They want a quick fix, especially those of us in the Western Hemisphere. If it's not Burger King, if we can't do it our way, we don't want it. Well, that's not the way listening works.

Listening isn't about you, really. It's about the other person. And out of that, you get you. That is what most people aren't clear about. Out of empowering another, you empower yourself. It isn't "either/or," it's an "and" conversation.

John: Can you say more about "and conversations" without feeling like you haven't told me enough?

Carol: One of the theories that quantum physicists are using is that we have lived in an either/or, black or white world. What the scientists are proving now is that the world is an "and" world. Up and down, hot and cold, right and left exist simultaneously. We live in a paradoxical world that encompasses opposites.

We have both sides to our humanness: the light and the dark, the good and bad, the front and the back. Most of us have been raised in a world that is either/or. Either you have a front or you have a back. I think that's a pretty funny concept, to have just a front and pretend you don't have a back. What do you call what's behind you? Often we only present our front; we don't show our back, which is supposed to be the *bad* stuff.

You are both. You have both. You are powerful and gentle and considerate and caring and loving, and you are also stingy, weak, cold, careless. You can also be treacherous. We have *both* as human beings. The ideal is to live from your strengths and to work diligently to minimize those things that are not in your best interests. I didn't say get rid of them. I said minimize. Don't live from there. Stop living and listening to the thought that you are all these bad things. Listen to other people, listen to yourself as the light side of yourself, as the bright side of yourself.

John: We're back to choice again. Always having a choice.

Carol: Always.

John: One of the things that occurred to me when you were speaking, Carol, is about this drama cycle. I'm not certain about mine. Obviously I have one. It has to be around anger. I know the end of it: I quit. I disappear. I go away. Or I disappear the other person. I am going to do whatever I have to do to stop being helpless.

There is a lot of upset that passes for relationships. When I am in a drama cycle, I am not making choices. I am angry because I am not being listened to, so I'm not in a great space to make a conscious choice.

Carol: Remember that one powerful tool we have is to stop ourselves, to say "wait." You see, we do have that ability to stop ourselves, although very few of us exercise it. We don't take the time to stop, back off, to say wait a minute, I am not in a place to talk about this right now. I am going to take five minutes, five hours, five days, or five weeks.

John: It requires quite a presence of mind. I guess it's the result of training. You have to train yourself to do that.

Carol: Ah, yes. Self-discipline. It's worth it, though. It's worth every moment that you spend on it.

Five

The Nine Disciplines of Listening

John: You know, discipline is one of those words like responsibility. You want to run from it. You say discipline, and I think the vast majority of people go south.

Carol: That is true, John. I hear that a great deal. I used to hate the "D word" as well. I couldn't even say it. Now I know that there is so much freedom in discipline. I know that sounds paradoxical. But when I am disciplined, I'm freed up to do things spontaneously.

For example, I have disciplined myself to listen to my mother from a place of empowerment. I now get to be very spontaneous with her. Because I've disciplined myself to listen to her in that way, I can be very playful and free with her. I find her delightful. She is very savvy and knowledgeable at eighty-two. That is very different from how I used to listen to her, which was, "She is old. She doesn't know anything. She is on the way out."

So everything she said was an irritant.

John: That was all in the way you listened to her?

Carol: Absolutely. My mother would call me in Jamaica and ask me if my night light was on because she was concerned about my being in a foreign country. She didn't want me to be hurt. When I was listening to her as this old, crochety woman, her words irritated me. Now I listen to her as a very capable, very loving, witty woman who cares.

John: When you mentioned that the result of discipline is freedom, that connects with something that you spoke about earlier in terms of the Zen of listening. I still don't understand how play and discipline come together—they seem antithetical.

Carol: They are. You need to do it with a consistency, with an intended purpose of play. "I am going to learn something about this and I am going to lighten up about it. I am going to be playful about it." If you approach it from a light-hearted purposeful intent, you can begin to discipline yourself to take on a particular way of being.

John: Are there other disciplines in listening that we can learn about and use?

Discipline #1: Practice Intuition

Carol: We have talked about intuition and how you learn to play with your intuition. You can play by intuiting who is on the telephone or at the front door. Learning to listen to that still, small voice. Intuition is a place for you to play, and yet you are putting in a discipline for beginning to trust something about yourself. If the word *discipline* bothers you, take it out. Say, "I am going to play. This is one of the ways that I play." You are going to put that play into a consistent pattern, and before you know it, you're doing something that is really a discipline. You have disciplined yourself to pay attention to your intuition.

John: So there is the discipline of intuition. What are some others?

Discipline #2: Being Heard

Carol: There is the discipline of being heard, making sure that you communicate in a way that you are heard. That one seems to be paradoxical. If I'm being heard, does that mean I'm talking or does that mean I'm listening? It means, John, that you're speaking to the person across from you in a way that they know *they're* being heard; therefore *you* are being heard. When you want to be heard, you listen first. Then you speak to what the person has said, not what you think they want to hear, which is what we generally do. When we speak to what people are saying, we are heard.

For example, when you said to me, "Say more about that," I would speak my drama cycle. At the end of it, you could say something like, "Wow, now that was very useful in terms of looking at my own drama cycle." What I get is that I said it and got heard, because you gave me the feedback about the contribution it made to you. Because I was heard, I listened to you and heard your question, with my machinery/internal dialogue out of the way.

Am I being clear?

John: I think so. I understand very clearly that human beings are reciprocal. If I am listening to you, that is a very strong step I can take to have you listen to me. Does the "discipline of being heard" mean I'm responsible for making sure I am heard?

Carol: Yes. It's a two-step process. First I listen. Then I speak to what I have heard. And if I'm not certain that you understood the message I want you to get, then I check with you. "Did I make myself clear?" Like I did just now.

John: Can we ask somebody to listen to us?

Carol: Yes. And you can also ask someone, "How do you want me to listen to you? Do you want me to listen to you without any comments? Do you want me to listen to you and give you feedback? Do you want me to brainstorm? Do you want me to give you my observations? Do you want me to make comments?" That way people know how to be with you. And, John, when people are asked so they are given a choice, they usually will tell you *exactly* what they want.

John: I am thinking of people who have spoken to me that way. They have almost an intimidating directness. I remember some personal growth and development workshops. Werner Erhard of est used to be very direct like that. It was a little off-putting, which was my listening evidently, right?

Carol: Yes.

John: Well, this discipline is certainly one I can try with my children, because sometimes I absolutely don't feel heard and I'm sure it's the same for them. I wonder, now, what would happen if my eleven-year-old son came to me and said, "Dad, I want you to listen to me this way."

Carol: John, think about what it would be like if a parent said to a child, "I want you to know that I am always going to hear you as a very capable, loving, competent human being. You will make mistakes because you're learning. I am always going to hear you as a capable, loving, competent human being." Look at the freedom this offers! "I am going to speak to you as a person who is capable, competent, and loving. When you do things that are contrary to that, I'm going to bring that to your attention. And that's the only way I am going to speak to you."

How do you think that child's listening would be for you as a parent?

John: Extraordinary. Of course, right now, I'm reflecting on my own carelessness when I (a) have not listened in that way and (b) have raised my voice because I felt helpless. You know I tried to push my agenda with them because it was good for them or whatever other silly reason.

Carol: Look at marriages, look at relationships. Look at friends and business associates. The only way you're going to listen to them or speak to them is as people who are capable, competent, and excellent. And when they don't act that way, you will bring it to their attention by saying: "I listen to you as capable, competent, and excellent, and I don't think you want me to think any other way. Does this represent what you want me to think or how you want me to listen?"

You don't reprimand them. You simply bring to their attention how you listen to them. This is *very* different from what we are used to.

John: Yes. This brings back something we mentioned a little earlier—about how you can literally "listen" people into increased leadership, increased capability, greater success. It's certainly a fascinating notion. Can I actually listen to you in such a way that your income goes up?

Carol: Yes, you can.

John: Now *there* is something to play with.

Carol: When I taught French in junior high school, I would get students who had been told by other teachers that they were C students at best. These children would show up as A students in my French class because I held them as competent, capable students able to learn a foreign language. We had a great time. They got A's because I would listen to them that way. I know it works. You can listen people to their greatness. You empower them.

John: That's a strong personal example for me because my listening for myself is that it isn't possible for me to learn a foreign language; hence I haven't learned one.

What other disciplines, Carol?

Discipline #3: Being Bold

Carol: There is a listening discipline called being bold. Being direct, willing to speak the truth as you see at that moment. It requires taking a risk—I will risk what you may think of me. I will risk your condemnation, I will take the risk that you are going to come back and bite me.

You will risk what you think of yourself in that process as well. So being bold is being authentic in the moment.

John: People are most uncomfortable with this one.

Carol: Yes, they are. However, countless lives have been saved by being bold in the moment.

John: Say more about that.

Carol: I'll give an example. There was a woman who was a very dear friend of mine. I knew that her relationship with her husband was less than desirable for her. I loved her and I loved him. She would come to me and complain about the things he did. I remember sitting down one day and saying

69

to her, "I have something to tell you. We may lose our relationship over this, and I'm much more concerned about *your* well-being than I am about my relationship with you. I think you're hurting yourself by staying there. You need to leave."

She gasped, "What do you mean? You've been agreeing with me all this time."

I said, "No, I haven't. You thought I was agreeing. What I have been doing is listening to you, and now it's time for me to speak to you truthfully. I think you are in a self-destructive relationship and that you need to get out. That's what I think and I'm no longer willing to sit by and listen to what you have to say. If you aren't going to do something about it, I no longer want to hear it."

That was bold. She huffed and she puffed and she was angry with me. She left. Later, she called back and thanked me. Six months later she left her husband. Our relationship became even closer because I had said something that was bold. I could no longer sit and listen to how her husband was being verbally abusive to her.

John: So this discipline of being bold has a great deal to do with courage.

Carol: It has *everything* to do with courage—the willingness to take the risk to empower someone through what you see and hear. That wasn't my opinion. I had enough feedback from her to know what he was doing. She kept going back, putting herself back in that situation. She might as well have been telling me, "I keep putting my hand on the hot stove." At some point I needed to say, "You're going to burn your hand off." That's not my opinion. That is a fact.

John: Carol, how do you distinguish between the *facts* and an *opinion?* Aren't all facts open to some interpretation? You spoke about physicists, and I know that in experiments they have begun to realize that the scientist, herself or himself, influences the outcome of the experiment. Also, no matter what the data, interpretation is involved. So how do you make that distinction between an opinion and what is so?

Carol: What is so is the information that the person has given you—what you've been told—the actual incident that has happened. Let's take this example of my friend again. She says that when she goes home at five o'clock at night, he's sitting at the dinner table with a knife and fork and a plate and pounding on the table, saying, "My dinner is not ready." When she goes by, he reaches out and jabs her with a fork. That is the fact I hear. So I can confidently say to her, "It's self-destructive to let somebody jab you with a fork. You've told me what is happening. You've told me how many times it has happened. You are crying about it. Yet you are going back into that situation." That is not my *opinion;* that is a *fact.*

John: Having listened to you, I'm clear you're not going to tell me that opinions are right or wrong. But how do we offer up an opinion in conversation so that it's listened to for what it is and isn't threatening, dangerous, or detrimental?

Carol: You make it an offering. Very often people give you their opinion as fact, the "only way" to do something. You can offer your opinion as your perspective of something, such as, "This is my perspective. Use it as you see fit." That allows people to hear your opinion, then take it or leave it.

John: Is there a difference between perspective and opinion and interpretation, or is that all one and the same thing?

Carol: In the listening work that I do, I hold it as all the same thing. In listening, the idea is to step back and be unattached to your opinion, perspective, interpretation. Be unattached from it and listen unconditionally to what the person is saying, holding the thought that they are capable and that you respect them.

John: Do you do this all the time? Or do you ever fall off the wagon and think somebody is an idiot?

Carol: Quite frequently. Then I'm clear that I'm back in my reactive lazy listening. Sometimes I'll even go there because it's fun. For example, there are times when I have a great deal of fun in my car. When people cut in front of me and run lights, I have the thought, *You jerk. That was really an idiot thing to do.* I'm clear that I'm just spouting off. They are my reactive thoughts and I'm playing with them.

John: But you save that for being alone in your car and not out in public, whacking people around with your listening.

Carol: Yes, I work very diligently at that because the minute I get lazy, the minute I let down that discipline, then I have what I call a "whack-a-do." That's when I hurt people with my listening. I am very clear about the power of listening. Now that I'm aware of the power of this tool, I no longer have the luxury to be careless with it. It's like a constant self-discipline. When you master listening, people truly trust you. You create that safe listening for everyone.

John: So much of personal growth and development and transformation is all about the monumental changes we need to make in ourselves. Listening seems like a really simple, non-threatening, less-complicated, easy adjustment to make.

Carol: It is. And it's so loving, so intimate, and so very rewarding.

John: How is it loving?

Carol: When you listen to someone unconditionally, you have placed no expectations, no condemnation, no judgment on them. When all that is missing, what is left is love. Listening it is one of the pure forms of love. I don't have to fall in love with you. I love you the way I love roses, or ice cream, or blue skies, or the Bahamas. I love you as I am listening. We demonstrate love and we don't ever have to meet again. In that moment, we have had a human experience of love.

I don't love what hate groups stand for. Yet, when I really hear the pain and fear in the people who participate in these, I can love the humanity in them. I'm not going to be stupid enough to put myself in their way either, and still I can see that they are very frightened, very disturbed, very angry because of early life decisions.

John: When you're listening in the way that you've been speaking about, are you automatically loving at the same time?

Carol: Yes. I'm loving you when I'm listening, and I never have to say "I love you." I just say, "Thank you." And people get it. Listening is love.

John: Carol, we have talked about the disciplines of intui-

73

tion, of being heard, of being bold. What are some other ones?

Discipline #4: Silence

Carol: There's silence. Although people don't think of silence as a discipline, it takes a great deal of discipline to be quiet. Silence is where you hear what people are *not* saying. So it's really in the silence that there's the most communication. Frequently in communication, people will use language to cover up what they are *not* saying. There is a way of listening that's deep enough to hear someone's silence, and in the silence you will hear their restlessness. You will hear a person's discomfort. You will hear their anguish.

John, I think you may relate to this in terms of your writing. When you write, you go off into another state. You're not all busy inside. You bring yourself to your writing with a certain purpose, intensity, and focus. There is no clutter going on around you. Is that not so?

John: Yes, for me. I don't even play music when I write. Silence is the context. In fact, I often find that I'm oblivious to the world around me when I am writing. It's not some artistic fit of temperament; it's a kind of focus.

Carol: That's silence, yes. Silence is something we need to give ourselves on a daily basis, and we usually don't. We need to withdraw from the noise of the world so that we can hear our own internal silence. It's like returning to an inner sanctuary. In that silence, you will hear clearly the still, small voice—your intuition. Silence will strengthen your intuition. Out of your silence, you will hear the noise of others. You'll actually be able to pick up their restlessness, their

74

concerns. I'm not talking about mind-reading. I am talking about picking up the energy, if you will, the noise that is coming from unspoken words, things that people haven't communicated. You will pick up the restless energy around them.

John: I'm a little baffled by how you hear unspoken words. Is it pure energy?

Carol: It's more like the rustling of trees. When you're out in open space, and it's very quiet, you can hear the silence of the wind. It's silent and yet you hear sound. Well, there is sound when people aren't saying something. You can hear the sound in the silence.

John: Simon and Garfunkel are right. You can hear the "sounds of silence." I would imagine that my silence is also a contribution to you as the speaker.

Carol: Absolutely. Because, in your silence, I get to hear what I'm saying—maybe for the first time. Since I'm not working with your "noise," I'm able to silence myself so that I'm not working to be heard. I'm not trying to prove I need to be heard. I'm actually resting, being able to come to my own sanctuary, my own silent place, and then hear what I have to say and speak from there.

Silence is a tool, a discipline that I support people in having every single day, a minimum of three times a day. I mean long periods of silence. I usually recommend that people go away for an entire weekend and have silence. There's a reason why the monks in the different monasteries have long periods of silence. It is a self-discipline tool. At minimum, we can do it just before we go to sleep.

John: Does silence stop the drama cycle when it is going on?

Carol: The perfect intervention is silence. If you want to stop a drama cycle, be silent. Do not interact with it. Allow the other person to do whatever they are doing around the drama cycle.

John: Have you observed that people have an intolerance for silence?

Carol: Oh, yes.

John: Where does that come from?

Carol: Intolerance comes from having to fill in the spaces. Always having to look like we're active. It's part of the automatic, reactive pattern or system of behaviors that we have put together. We feel we have to stay moving. When people cannot be with silence, they really don't want to hear their own sadness, or their own anger. Or how they may have let themselves down in some way. I have heard people say over and over again, "I can't be with myself. I just can't be alone."

Silence as a discipline is a tool for you to renew and rejuvenate yourself. It's also a tool to re-invent yourself. What I mean by re-invent is to update those decisions that you made as a child with little to no information about how the world really is. In silence you can get back in touch with who you really are and then re-invent yourself, update yourself.

John: As you were speaking, one of the things that occurred to me was a concern I've had about my kids. My daughter is sixteen. My son is eleven. They have a tremendous intolerance for silence. The music is on or the TV is on or they're with somebody or they're on the phone. It seems from the moment they awake to the moment they go to bed, there is something going on. I know that's what kids do, but I'm concerned about that because I have always found that the ability to sit and think was one of the most cherished things that I did. Even when I'm as busy as I have ever been, I always made time for that cup of coffee on the porch by myself. Just think, just look, just do nothing. Watch the birds. The older I get, the more I crave that time, the more comfortable I am with that time.

Carol: I think you've hit on a good point about teenagers. The need for stimuli during our pubescence has a lot to do with all of the activity that is going on with us internally: hormone changes and other aspects of growing up. Bringing in all the stimuli around us is part of finding out who we are. That need for stimuli is intensified if we have parents or other adults who don't listen to us.

We can support teenagers through this transitional time by really listening to them and having them experience being heard. If we can give that to our teenagers, they wouldn't need a lot of this loud music. They are in the process of being recognized, being experienced. That is what a lot of the stimuli is about.

John: Is it possible that music is so loud they couldn't hear me anyway?

Carol: It's very possible. When you start to put silence into practice, though, they will start to hear the sounds of silence.

John: You spoke about hearing what isn't being said, and made the distinction between that and mind-reading. Can we distinguish the discipline of silence more than that?

Carol: When people speak and you're listening to them, you can sometimes tell that there's uneasiness in both speaker and listener. It's almost as if you're anticipating something else. They keep talking and you keep waiting for something else. Many of us have had that experience because we know something has gone unsaid. Whatever it was they were attempting to communicate, it didn't get communicated.

John: Would that be true whenever we had a sense of not being complete with a conversation?

Carol: Yes. You can tell when something is missing.

John: Okay. What other disciplines are there? We've talked about being heard, intuition, being bold, and silence.

Discipline #5: Brevity

Carol: My favorite discipline is brevity: be brief, get to the point, and say what there is to say. Mean what you say and say what you mean. Most of us think, "If I say what I mean, you're going to ask me for an explanation." That is not so when you say *exactly what you mean,* as long as the listener is listening to you. If the listener is judging, evaluating, condemning, analyzing, they are not listening. You can expect a request for explanation as a possible response when the other person isn't really listening.

When you say what you mean and you mean what you say, it cuts to the quick of communication. You are complete, and so is the true listener. When you are brief, when you have said it all, there is nothing else to say. It's wise to know when that happens.

John: I'm a writer, and writers are sometimes paid to say a great deal about very little. So I have been schooled to do that. But in speaking to people, I have tried to catch myself and make a choice. But then I would say things in such detail or two or three different ways because I really just didn't trust that the person would get it. I would explain it again and again and again because I didn't trust that you would understand it. Which is, once again, all about me, and has nothing to do with you. Is that common?

Carol: Yes. Mine would be that I wouldn't think I was enough. It's that early decision again. When I'm listening, and the person is saying something over and over, I'll ask them, "Did I get what you wanted me to get? Did I hear what you wanted me to hear?" Saying that brings them present again.

John: When I talk too much, say something over and over, it's a funny, complicated thing: my listening for my assumption about your listening.

Carol: Yes. You have already assumed something about how I'm going to listen, how the world is going to listen to you. So you go on and on. People who do that haven't bothered to check to see how the person in front of them is listening. It's true that the person may have checked out a long time ago. They are not around to find out, because *they've* already determined how it is. So it's like two ships passing in the night. We are not having the same conversation.

John: Language is remarkable, and what we're talking about here is language both in speaking and in listening. Brevity might be difficult for me because I have such a love of words.

Carol: You have a way of being precise, John, and when you are precise, that is brevity. It's when you want to expand on your preciseness that the brevity stops.

John: Okay. Let's go on to other disciplines, Carol.

Discipline #6: The 99/1 Rule

Carol: Another discipline is one that I've called the "99/1 Rule." Let's take the drama cycle again. You said, "Say more about that, Carol." And I'm thinking, "Oh, goodness, I didn't say enough." I'm going through my drama cycle, with all your expressions seeming to confirm that I need to do more. The 99/1 Rule says that whatever is going on here is going on with me as I'm going through my drama cycle. All you did was sit with a particular look on your face and I was off and running. You're only one percent of this.

John: So it's 99 percent you, one percent me?

Carol: Right. That one percent, that word or tone of voice, was enough for me to take that as my trigger and run my drama cycle. Now, the same applies to you. I could be in my drama cycle and you could be listening to me as I'm explaining something. In my drama cycle, I could say, "It always ticks me off when you scratch your forehead like that, John. It upsets me when you do that." You were perfectly fine before I said that. Now that may trigger something in you. You may feel unjustly accused.

80

John: It seems that drama cycles love the company of other drama cycles.

Carol: Absolutely. You can't play by yourself. That's why the 99/1 Rule works so well. If you're just sitting there listening, the person going through a drama cycle will finally burn themselves out. They do one of two things: they really get that it is all over, that they don't have to continue, or they will find somebody else to play with.

Some people marry each other because their drama cycles are compatible. For example, if I am "not enough" and you are weak and helpless and we get married, we can just play that one out for the next forty-nine years.

Why would we do this? Why would we spend our lives playing out our drama cycles? We'd do it because then we wouldn't have to contribute our gifts or talents to the world. We don't have to live from our vision, from our excellence. We get to go through life caught up in our drama cycles.

John: But, Carol, I can't believe that people wouldn't want to contribute their gifts.

Carol: It's a way to avoid responsibility, John. It's a big responsibility to live up to our excellence, our magnificence. It means we don't have the luxury of being lazy. We don't have the luxury of not following through. We don't have the luxury of any more excuses. It means we now need to be responsible for what comes out of our mouth and for how our life looks. It's so much easier to hang our hats on Mom, Dad, the principal, the policeman, the condition of society. Blaming everything on others is much easier.

Pulling yourself up by your bootstraps is difficult. Look at our Secretary of State, Madeleine Albright. She could have said, well, I am an immigrant, or my parents were this and my parents were that, so I can't make it. That is obviously not what she did. She moved forward. She lived true to her vision, true to her excellence and her gifts. We all have the capability.

John: So the listening that occurred around that woman was "Anything is possible. Strive, achieve, etc." That was the listening context that she grew up with.

Carol: Yes. That is the listening.

John: Often I have heard people say that we are simply mirrors for each other and the problem I have with you is really a problem in me. The objection I have about you is something that I'm seeing in myself. Is that part of the 99/1 Rule?

Carol: Sometimes it is. I would say that to the degree that you react to the person's drama cycle, there is something still within you that you haven't resolved. To the degree that you have resolved it, you are no longer a mirror for me. So you can scratch your forehead and I won't think I'm not enough; I'm clear that I am, and that I'm not stupid. I have resolved that in myself. Now, if I say it upsets me every time you scratch your forehead, to the degree that you haven't resolved being tricked and set up, you will think I attacked you.

John: So any time I'm getting hot about something, that should be a real red flag to me that I can bring in the discipline, the tool, of 99/1. I can begin to shift my listening because I know I'm plugged into something and not really listening.

Carol: Yes.

John: Couples are masterful at knowing how to throw 99/1 where it doesn't belong.

Carol: So are children. They know exactly how to trigger parents. Teenagers are really masterful at it.

John: Is this just sport for people? I mean, what are they doing this for?

Carol: I really don't think it's sport, John. There is a physiological condition that happens when we get into our drama cycle. It releases toxins into our blood system. We actually get addicted to the chemicals that go into our body when we're upset.

John: Like with alcohol or nicotine?

Carol: Yes. It's an addictive behavior. The minute you start practicing the discipline of empowered listening, you break that cycle of the toxins going into your system and you begin to step up the flow of endorphins. It's just like running every day. You know the difference between when you've had your endorphins kick in and when they don't. You could feel sluggish and worn and tired, yet if you make yourself run, you get those endorphins flowing and, all of a sudden, wow—you're wide awake again. Well, the same thing happens when you practice the discipline of empowered listening. You say, "I'm not going to do that. This is how I'm going to hold this situation." All of a sudden, you wake up. You've started to create an energy flow, endorphins going into your blood system.

People can get addicted to endorphins as well as toxins. Which would you rather have: toxins or endorphins?

Frankly, I'd rather create the discipline of having endorphins flowing into my system than having toxins in my body.

John: Carol, we've covered a number of disciplines. Are there any more in this Zen of listening?

Discipline #7: Acknowledgment

Carol: Acknowledgment is another one, John. You know, by the time we're five years old, we know how to automatically say, "Thank you" and "Please" and "I'm sorry." Those "acknowledgments" are so automatic and unconscious, they've lost their meaning. We say all that without really being present to what we're saying. However, the acknowledgment that I'm talking about as a discipline is to really communicate to the person the contribution they've made to you by listening to you and by speaking to you. We don't usually acknowledge people for that. We don't say, "Thank you for that contribution. It allowed me to see how, as a three-year-old, I felt betrayed. And how I have carried that forward."

John, had you not shared that four-year-old story with me, I wouldn't have taken a deeper look at what happened to me with Miss Tina and my school lunch, and how all that has set a pattern through my life. I've given that some thought. That was a contribution to me. It gave me additional places to look: where else in my life am I carrying around this three-year-old behavior I don't even know I'm doing? I thank you.

How often do people thank you that way, John? How often do you thank people that way? Acknowledgment as a discipline takes a concentrated effort. You have to look for and then thank the person for the contribution that they've made to you in the communication—in the listening *and* in the speaking.

I'm not saying we don't need to be trained, as children, to have appropriate behavior. What I am saying is that what we often do is slip into what's automatic and comfortable, what's easy, and what's going to cause the least amount of trouble. We're putting ourselves on automatic, which can be good when you're driving a car; not so good when talking to people.

John: The image I have is the classic 1960s TV family with the husband and the newspaper. "Yes, dear. That's nice, dear." There's no relationship going on there at all. How do you bring that present, Carol? How do you make the "thank you" real?

Carol: One way is to establish eye contact. I don't mean the 1980 California eye contact, when people would look you dead in the eyes and nobody would be home. I mean an actual contact with someone. Looking at them and very quickly, concisely, with brevity, saying, "Thank you," making sure the person got it. That acknowledgment only takes thirty seconds, if that long. However, we usually don't take those few seconds to establish eye contact with someone. We look away, we look down; we do something else.

Another way to acknowledge someone is to reach out and gently touch either their hand, arm, or shoulder. You can do this when you say "Please" so that they know that it's authentic for you. That it's truly a request coming from authenticity and sincerity.

"I'm sorry" is one thing that's so automatic. We say "I'm sorry" for just about everything. I'm sorry I coughed. I'm sorry my dandruff got on my shoulder. I'm sorry I'm sorry. I take exception to the automatic-ness. I think "I'm sorry" ought to really mean you're sorrowful. I think there's a way to simply acknowledge that you did something. You can say, "Excuse me." Or "Pardon me for having done that."

Here's a story I like: When my mother would go down the hall to her office every day, she'd have to pass by the office of a co-worker. Every morning the co-worker would yell out, right on schedule, "Hi, Lucy. How are you?" My mother would say, "I'm fine," and the woman would say, "That's great!" One day my mother was determined to stop this automatic question, so when the woman said, "How are you?" my mother replied, "I died." The woman replied, "That's great!" Then she looked up and said, "Oh." She realized she wasn't home.

John: Is it fair to play with people like that?

Carol: I think so. It's a wake-up call. If you really want to know how I am, hang around to hear the answer. If you don't care about the answer, don't ask the question. You can always just say, "Hi, I hope you have a great day."

John: Sometimes I really want acknowledgment and yet, when I get it, I'm uncomfortable. It's awkward and I run away from it. It's sort of crazy. When I get a really flowery introduction, it's always hard to just be content to say, "Thank you."

Carol: It's great to embrace and master "Thank you." Nothing else is required. When you start to give acknowledgments, and you start to receive them, that skill of saying, "Thank you," and just letting it be, grows stronger.

One way you can start to get comfortable with acknowledgments is by going into agreement. I say, "John, that is a great shirt you're wearing." You respond, "Yes, it's wonderful. I got it when I was in India and I really like the fabric." Really get into it, so you become accustomed to standing in the presence of acknowledgment. Eventually you're comfortably with receiving an acknowledgment because you participated in it. That may take time. Then you'll be able to say, "Oh, thanks" and that's it.

John: One of the themes you constantly bring me back to is that I am responsible for my life. The business about acknowledging the shirt is like, "Oh, you mean I'm responsible for the richness of my life?"

I know how important acknowledgment can be in business. Talk to me about going beyond "thank you" and "please" in terms of acknowledging people in that context.

Carol: When you leave out that important factor of acknowledgment, people's productivity and your profitability will drop because people want to be recognized for what they have contributed. Powerful leaders know this. They very skillfully and quite naturally do this. Notice I didn't say they *automatically* do this. They have deliberately put into place two powerful components of leadership. One is the skill of listening—really listening, to what the speaker, the client, the salesperson, or the customer wants. Not listening to their own agenda.

The second is acknowledging the contribution that the person has made to the company, to the organization, to the overall picture. This can be done with rewards such as bonuses or dividends, something that goes beyond what the person expects. People love perks, and a skilled leader knows that, and keeps those components active in their interactions with people all the time.

John: Is there a particular way, Carol, that you're recommending we acknowledge people? I noticed, for instance, that when you acknowledged me in the four-year-old story, you were specific about what that contribution was.

Carol: I'm certainly recommending that you be specific because to acknowledge someone for "your contribution" leads them to wonder, What did I do? And specific acknowledgment validates that what they did was very appropriate for you, and they get to revisit the gift of that contribution. Also, very often it will encourage people to speak. I heard one person say, "You know, I used to hold back what I had to say because I thought people wouldn't get anything from what I said. Then I got feedback from people in this group that what I said meant something to them. So now I'm going to speak up all the time." When you give people feedback about the contribution that they made to you, it empowers them to continue to speak and to continue to give their ideas, their insights, their life experiences as a contribution.

John: When I want recognition and then stand up on a stage in front 500 people and get it, I feel awkward, which is that childhood stuff coming up. However, when someone specifically says, "You know, John the contribution that you've made to me is this, and thank you," it's hard to do mischief with that.

Carol: Yes, that's a good point; it really does keep you out of that "mischief" as you call it. It brings you present, no matter what's going on with you in terms of your listening about yourself. Here's someone who finds you valuable in a specific way, and your early childhood decisions can't invalidate that. It gets dissipated.

John: Are there any systematic approaches to keep this acknowledgment really present, to remind yourself constantly to do it? I know that, as an owner of a company, I forget. It's not that I don't appreciate the contribution that the men and women I work with are giving, but in the day-to-day business, I forget.

Carol: Yes, there is a systematic way to do this, and I do recommend this to people regularly: give a minimum of five acknowledgments a day. That's to begin developing the muscle of the discipline of acknowledgment. As long as you do your five, it doesn't matter what they are. However, there is a condition: they cannot be to the same person. You have to give acknowledgments to five *different* people. You don't get to cheat on this one; you do need to stretch that muscle. Giving acknowledgments is awkward, and it's a discipline well worth mastering. Be present to those five, and be authentic.

A simple example would be "John, thank you for bringing me coffee this morning. I walked out of the house without my coffee, and your bringing me the coffee reminded me of when my mother would bring me my hot oatmeal. So thank you, that's a huge contribution; it brought back to me the fun I used to have as a child." In that instant, your acknowledgment tells something about me and something about you. We connected, and how long did that take? A few seconds. It's a great interchange—it empowered you and it empowered me. We became at ease with each other in a very short time.

I make a distinction between compliment and acknowledgment. Going back to the shirt from India, a compliment would be, "It's a great shirt, John," period. However, "That's a great shirt, John, is it from India?" is more of an acknowledgment. The difference is that I'm really present and involved in your shirt and you.

John: Does acknowledgment have to do with intention?

Carol: Yes, it does. If your intention in acknowledgment is to empower somebody, then you need to be fully present for those few seconds. Otherwise you're just trying to look polite. I know that most people are well intentioned, but they're not present—they don't remain present to the desired outcome of the conversation. They aren't clear about the end result. Most people speak hoping the other person gets it rather than paying attention to the listener to see if he or she is getting it! They go through the motions. They want it all to happen automatically. Personal development through listening takes work, and it's well worth mastering.

There are a lot of people who think they're quite far underway with this development. Many people in the helping professions, people like psychiatrists and psychologists and social workers who work with people, say, "I already know how to listen." They do listen, and they listen with an agenda. I'm talking about an agenda-less listening. I'm talking about agenda-less acknowledgment. There isn't anything behind it other than an acknowledgment that the person has been a contribution to you, and you have received something out of the interaction. Most trained professionals are trained to listen with a specific purpose. And for the purposes for which they've been trained, that's appropriate. For general interaction between two human beings, however, it doesn't work.

John: Certainly for a salesperson or a manager who's having an interaction with an employee or employees, there must be many times when an agenda is required.

Carol: Yes, and since you have an agenda, what is yours? Is your agenda to empower them to get this particular job, project, sale, whatever it is, accomplished? The bottom line is to have you and the other person in partnership to have this happen. Now how do we go about meeting that agenda? One of the key tools is to listen. Listen to see how far off the mark is the customer, the employee, the salesperson. Between where they are and where you both want to get to, what's missing?

Not what's *wrong*—what's *missing* so we can put it in, so you can get there so that can happen. That's a worthwhile agenda, because it's a win-win. If your agenda is to have things done *your* way, however, that totally cuts out the other person, and takes effort and struggle.

What works is an "and conversation," the one we talked about before. How do you *and* I win at the same time? It's a form of teamwork. Because I listened, I heard what's important. I coach people to ask their colleagues, "How do I best work with you? Do I check in once a day, once a week, three times a week? Are you a person who needs direct management, or do you prefer to have some guidance and then go off and do it yourself? Do I just tell you that this is the end result, leave you alone, and check in with you periodically for a status review?" Very few people ask that question, "How do I best work with you?" If you do, you can listen to their need to be empowered in a certain way. Most people aren't going to tell you unless you ask. You're really asking, "How do I empower you? How do we get you to be profitable and productive in your style, so that I can match my style with yours?"

John: When you have an agenda, do you make it clear up front?

Carol: Yes. You can say, "Look, this is what I'm after. I'm very eager that this week we come in at $40,000 in sales, and I want your partnership in doing this. Now, I know that you are here, you've been doing this, you've been talking with this many people (that's part of acknowledgment), and we're about $18,000 or $20,000 now. What do you see we can do to get to this $40,000 number between now and Friday? I'm so committed to our getting there, let's look and see what we need to do, and how often we need to check in. What do I need to do to support you?" People can get excited about that.

You've put your agenda out there. You've made it very clear what you're after and what you're committed to. You need to see if I'm on board with you. You want to find out what would be in this for me. We *both* are going to win here.

From this kind of conversation, people begin to jump on board. And if they say, "I don't see any way that I'm going to make it to that by the end of this week," you need to find out why. For example, listen for whether they're burned out. They may say, "Look, I've worked eight weeks straight, seven days in a row, I've had no time off." Ah, it's not that they aren't willing! You can now be in partnership with that person, now that you know something else is going on. It's not that they're not willing, they're exhausted. Okay. A different game plan is called for.

I don't care if your group is 70,000 strong; are you still in there keeping the tools sharp and listening? Keeping yourself masterful at what you're doing? Many leaders are not. They conduct workshops and share their expertise, but are they listening? That's the challenge for leaders and top producers.

I put myself in personal development work every year for ten days; in fact, this year I'm going to do it for ten weeks. Because, John, there's nothing people dislike more than a fraud. Someone who doesn't do what they're asking you to do. You have to live and walk your example, and acknowledge. Acknowledgment, recognizing people, is part of that, because you're in partnership.

Discipline #8: Empowerment of Others

Carol: Another discipline involves empowering others through coaching actions and listening community. We are a nation of what I call John Waynes and Jane Waynes. We do it ourselves. We are of the old pioneering stock: "I don't need your help, and I can run this all by myself." We are quite entrepreneurial, and we're proud of starting things and building things. What we forget is that we really didn't do it by ourselves. We did it with a team of people, and we've always needed others. A wagon train didn't consist of just one person. Besides that, neighbors would come and help you build your house; they would bring food over.

We all need coaches, and it is a discipline to bring coaches into your life. I have six coaches, one for each area of my life. I have a coach for my personal development and personal growth, I have a coach for my relationships, I have a coach for my career, I have a coach for my health. In fact, in some of those areas, I have two or three coaches. I know the areas where I'm most resistant. So, I have a community of coaches—people who are not attached to my results, though they are committed to my results.

What do I mean by that? They *champion* me. They want to see me make it. They're clear that I can be successful in anything that I take on, and I look to them to point out what I don't see. A non-attached coach is another pair of eyes who looks with me. I have my coaches brainstorm with me, I share my plans and strategize with them. I ask them, "What do you see in this? What are some of the pitfalls and where am I headed?"

It's interesting, John, that I choose people who are not my best friends, because I know they're going to tell me the truth. People who love me may not want to tell me the truth because they don't want to hurt my feelings, so those people are not my coaches. For example, in the area of health, where I'm the most resistant, I took on three people who have no problem telling me get it together. They say, "I'm really concerned about your health; you've got a lot of work to do. You need to handle this, this, and this. Have you started doing your exercises? You don't like to exercise? Do you like to dance? Do you like aerobics? What do you like?" They don't take no for an answer, and they don't take excuses. "When did you start? Did you do your fifteen minutes today?"

John: You've formalized these relationships?

Carol: Yes, I have. I have actually asked them, "Will you coach me in these areas? Will you be rigorous with me? Will you hold me accountable in these areas?" And they do. Why do I need somebody to hold me accountable? Because I'm all over the planet, I am literally all over the globe, and it's easy for me to scam out and not exercise. My coaches insist that I book myself into a hotel with gyms, equipment, treadmills, that has massages and spas and everything I need.

Make sure that your coaches know how to reach you and you know how to reach them. Formalize the agreement with these coaches to support you in absolutely accomplishing what you set out to accomplish.

John: Do you have regular appointments with these people?

94

Carol: I check in once a month with every single one of them. Right now I'm talking to one or another of my health coaches three times a week. I've set it up. I've said, "I need to do this with you for the next six to nine months," and they said, "Fine."

John: About three months ago, Susan and I hired a fitness coach and we know when he's going to come. The very fact that he's there means I have to show up. And I can see the results. That coaching relationship is a joy.

You said you have coaches in other areas. Do you have some requirements for choosing them—besides the fact that they have a discipline of being bold with you?

Carol: They are also people who demonstrate the accomplishment or the final result that I'm after. For example, in the area of finances, my coaches have actually walked their talk: they've invested wisely and purchased property. They have a great portfolio. All the things I don't know how to do. Now I'm beginning to step into handling my finances and setting up my retirement plan and a legacy for my children and grandchildren. I'm going to go to someone who's already encountered the obstacles that I know I will encounter, so they can coach me through them and also give me the insight and information that I don't have.

Another example is in the area of recreation. I have a friend who is absolutely one of the most playful people I have ever met. He lives in Jamaica. He has every water toy imaginable. He goes parasailing, he has a banana boat, he goes windsurfing, and he also has one of those open-air jeeps so he can go up into the mountains. When I'm in Jamaica, I go play with him. Also, he takes risks and knows how to do it safely. He checks things out, he makes sure that there's ample protection. He's an absolute joy, and he's is so thorough around playing that I know I'm going to be safe.

John: It sounds like your coaches keep you congruent with your commitment. Is that so?

Carol: That's absolutely right. A listening community keeps you congruent with who you are. It keeps you congruent with your vision, with your greater self. Your listening community is designed to keep you empowered. And you have the choice to put that into place. You can choose your listening community. I say you're missing the mark if you don't have at least six coaches. The more you have, the faster and more powerfully you'll get where you want to go.

John: I've hired professional "nags." I literally have employed, through various means, people who nag me. I realize I need to be prodded when I'm not doing something that is really best for me or I'm not keeping a commitment I've made to other people or to myself. I need somebody "in my face" to help me overcome my inertia. I'm not suggesting everybody does this, but I'll bet there are a couple of million people out there who really could use that kind of relationship.

In our company, we created a "Book of Nudge," a sort of financial challenge. It included all the things we would accomplish by a certain time, and we allocated the coaching relationship to what we called a "nudge coach." The nudge coach is to nudge us along, via e-mail or in conversations or on the phone.

For example: "John, you agreed to do this by the 24th. It's the 20th. How's it going?" On the 21st I got another call, and on the 22nd and 23rd I got calls. Well, oddly enough, I got it done. I'm getting them *all* done. One person in the organization is referred to as the "nudge queen." She keeps the Book of Nudge and she checks up on all the nudgers. It's fun. You don't have to be beaten up to move forward in your life.

I know in your courses you talk about having a partner for daily communication exercises. You're with that partner for fifteen or twenty minutes on the phone every morning and you go through a communication exercise, which really keeps you present to what's going on and things you've learned. I've tried it and found it tremendously beneficial. What about that in terms of listening community?

Carol: That kind of interaction on a daily basis is a way of establishing a listening community. Since I started my listening course back in May of 1995, there are people who are still talking to their original daily partners. If they're not talking to them on a daily basis, they're talking to them at least weekly. What happens in that kind of listening community is that there is a "safe sanctuary." That may sound redundant. But very often we don't make sure that our sanctuary is completely safe (with a person who can hear us unconditionally). The daily calls provide an unconditional way of being heard. They create a bond between you and that partner.

You can broaden your listening community with people who participated in the same listening course, or who are aware of the dynamic that occurs. You can extend it out to people who have always listened to you like that. There are people in our lives who have been waiting for us to understand that they have always been there for us. I like to say that they've been having a party, with horns and confetti and all that, waiting for us to show up for our birthday. There's the already-established listening community.

Do you know people who have always championed

you, who have always talked to you about how great you are? They've been in the wings, and you've never called on them and said, "I really want you as part of my listening community and this is what I need from you." What you want to tell them is, "I need you to listen to me unconditionally. I want you to hear what I have to say. And I want you to champion me and really support me in my success." They'll probably say, "I've been doing that."

John: You know, Carol, years ago you gave me an exercise that I'll never forget, though in my laziness I haven't done it recently. You told me to call five people, to tape the calls, and request of those people that for three minutes they tell me everything that they admired about me, respected about me, that I could be counted on for, that they were proud of me for doing and being and having. Three solid minutes of upbeat, positive strokes. No negativity, no criticism, no either/or allowed. I'll never forget that exercise. The first person that I did it with blew me away. At the time I was just facing a truckload of problems, and I wasn't doing well with any of them. I don't think I got to the second call before I was out of my defeatist mentality about it all. A very, very powerful thing.

Two things I want to bring up. One, which I'm sure most people don't know, is that you and I are on the phone every morning, going through a series of communication exercises with each other. The interesting thing is that these calls are outrageously intimate. I have said things to you that I've never said to another human being. I'm telling you the dearest little details, and I'd never had a chance to say these things before. The benefits of that are extraordinary. First, I get to say them, and second, I get to say them to someone I know with 100 percent surety will never use them against me. And here I am, the guy who doesn't trust!

The other thing is that it's marvelous training. Susan and I, for the first time in our relationship, sat down in front of the fireplace a number of nights ago and told each other a fantasy that we had. I'm way conservative to have these conversations normally. I don't think I would have been able to have that conversation with Sue if it weren't for the daily communication calls I have with you because, as you've said so often, it's a muscle I've been training.

Carol: Thank you, John.

John: You're welcome. Now, Carol, let's recap. We've covered eight of the nine disciplines so far. They are:

Practice Intuition
Being Heard
Being Bold
Silence
Brevity
The 99/1 Rule
Acknowledgment
Empowerment of Others

What's the final one? What's the ninth discipline?

Six

Final Words—Empowered Listening

Carol: Empowered listening is the umbrella discipline under which all the other disciplines fall. In order to do empowered listening, you need to have all nine disciplines. Empowered listening is only practical when it's integrated into your daily life. You and I can sit and talk about empowered listening and how you shift your listening around people; that's a great conversation, and that's what it remains until it's put into action. Empowered listening really needs to show up in your daily life.

What do you do when your wife Susan says, "John, I really hate it when you use that tone of voice?" When she says that to you, you have a choice. You can go to "I'm now being tricked. I'm now being set up." You can go to the place of that little child who was traumatized. You can use your lazy, reactive listening or you can go to the empowered listening place of, "I hold this woman as capable, competent, and loving, and I respect her. Okay, 99/1. Now, let me listen to what she's really saying to me." Holding that listening, and not reacting. Susan, through her own process, will say what she needs to say because you've really listened to her.

John: I've *empowered* her, instead of trying to *overpower* her.

Carol: Yes.

John: When she says, "I don't like it when you use that tone of voice," or "John, it's not what you say, it's how you say it," I used to consider that a battle cry, an invitation to slug it out. It's that automatic kind of thing I've watched myself do in the past.

Carol: That's what we tend to do in relationships. We do what we are "thrown to." Someone throws us something and we react. We don't employ the discipline of empowerment. We don't stop and say, "Okay, there's a message here. Something happened, and I'm going to empower this person so that I can hear what happened."

John: Yes. I'm getting clear that I need practice on the 99/1 discipline, so I can understand if what I've done with my tone of voice was to trigger something. And I'm not a bad person because I used that tone of voice. I don't need to beat myself up about what I just did. I can just say, "Oh, I triggered something in Sue" and simply listen.

Carol: John, I can share a first-hand experience of this. My children's father, my first husband, calls me Carol Ann, and he has a very authoritative way of speaking to me, even on the telephone when he calls to see how our adult children are doing. He says, "How are you doing, Carol Ann?" And he has *this tone*. For years, all I had to do was hear him call me Carol Ann and I was off and running, creating my own drama cycle. Since I've been practicing empowered listening, I can remember that Carol Ann is a very loving, kid-like name that my family uses. It was also a way to put me in place when I did something wrong. All my mother ever had to do when I was a little kid who had misbehaved is say, "Carol Ann." So that's how I hear it—uh oh, what have I done?

So I started to shift my listening. My ex-husband still says "Carol Ann," and he never changed his tone of voice. I changed my way of listening to how he said what he said. I now choose to hear that he respects me—I hear that because he's told me. I hear his concern for our children and wanting the very best for them. *And* he has this way of delivering his message. Period. Now I don't get triggered. I don't go off into my drama cycle. I'm able to stay on the phone and listen to this man deliver his message.

John: What happens when somebody who uses "Carol Ann" with you actually has the intention of putting you in your place?

Carol: Well, if that's the case, I will ask them, "What's your intended result? What is it you intend to happen between me and you by calling me that?" That's boldness—one of the disciplines. And if they have the boldness to tell me, "I think you ought to know that you did something wrong," I don't mind responding, "If I've done something unknowingly to you that has dishonored you, I ask you forgiveness. My intention is that we're both winning." I've done that, many, many times, John. Because there are times when I do things unknowingly. However, I'm not willing to have you make me wrong. If I dishonored you and I didn't know it, I'll clean it up. It's that simple. And it works every time.

For example, when I show up late, I don't say, "I'm sorry I'm late." I acknowledge that I'm late. I'm not sorrowful. In case anybody's interested in how come I'm late, I tell them the truth: "I didn't allow myself enough time to get here, and that won't happen again." Or, "I got a phone call the minute I was walking out the door that I did need to take." I'll tell them what happened and it's not an excuse.

I'm being responsible. I keep myself empowered in the presence of people who may, unknowingly, be out to disempower me. I'm unwilling to go into partnership with them to disempower me.

I take responsibility for being heard. I have to be heard—and so does the other person. I'm committed to *both* of us being heard. If I took a phone call that made me late and they feel dishonored, I heard them and we're both right. I know how to handle that the next time. I'll take the person's phone number, and if I'm going to be late, I'll call them on my car phone. I want to know what's going to work between the parties involved, and I won't know unless they tell me. If you tell me it doesn't work for me to be late, I won't be late for you, John.

John: Mostly you have to ask, because it's not something we tend to volunteer.

Carol: Yes, I can say, "I was late—did that cause you any problems? Did I in any way offend you?" That keeps us empowered.

You know, people do so many things to disempower others, and they're unaware of it. Take sales, for example. A sales person says to the customer, "I'd like you to consider this proposal or this product or this recommendation and get back to me." Then they leave out "by Thursday" or whenever. Why is that a disempowering thing? What's behind it?

John: I suppose it's fear of getting a "No" response. If I ask something so specific as, "Will you get back to me by Thursday at five o'clock?" that's an invitation for a negative response. So I'd rather put that off. I'll just pretend.

Carol: Exactly. What people forget is that it's also an invitation for a *positive* response. We don't usually think of that one. If you ask for a response by Thursday at five and the person says that won't work, you ask, "Why not?" The listening you may have is that you'll be rejected for being pushy. It's easier to live with a committed "maybe."

John: It's a "stay of execution" of sorts.

Carol: Yet it's very disempowering to you as the sales person as well as to the customer. We all need completions. The customer will be thinking, "I didn't get back to him with an answer. I didn't finish reading that proposal." Deadlines keep things moving forward. I like them. Not because they box me in, but because they're my benchmarks.

When Thursday at five o'clock comes, the customer can say, "You know, I'm not quite finished reading this proposal. I'll have it done tomorrow morning by eight; will that work for you?" I say, "Fine." Now we're back in communication. I have a listening that you can be responsible for what you commit to do. I listen to you that way.

The idea, the discipline, is to have an empowered listening for everyone you meet. Most people would say, "Oh, come on, that's six billion people. I can't possibly do that!" I said that myself fifteen years ago. I was skiing with a friend named Sally, who I thought was the best friend any human being could ever have. She was thoughtful, she listened—in fact she was the beginning of my listening community. Sally and I had just gotten off the ski lift and were having this great conversation and I said, "Sally, I just love being with you." And I had the thought, *Wouldn't it be great to love everybody like Sally?*

Now, I don't go around hearing voices, John. However, I heard a prophetic listening that said, "You will." I remember going down that slope yelling, "No, I can't love everybody like I love Sally!" Fifteen years later, I do, John. I absolutely do. How do I do that? I listen to them from a place of empowerment.

That's authentic for me. It took me fifteen years to get here, and I think it's well worth mastering that listening skill. It doesn't take any more effort for me to listen to you powerfully as it does to listen to Sally or Mark or Martha or anybody out there on the street. It's especially useful when you are upset with someone. The question I ask is, "What's the intention here? What is this person really trying to get me to understand?" That's so much easier than going off the handle. That doesn't mean I never get angry or upset—it means that when I do, I shift because I don't like that energy. I would much rather be in the place of, "Well, what's the message here?" I come out feeling taller and stronger, and so does the person with me. So we both win. That is the power of empowered listening.

John: You talked about being angry. Is anger always an indication that a drama cycle is going on?

Carol: Yes, it is.

John: Let's revisit the business of the drama cycle and how you use empowered listening to get out of it; also, how to recognize when someone else is in their drama cycle and what you can do to bring them out of it. I have a feeling the drama cycle is the key to a lot of empowered listening.

Carol: There are three things that happen in anybody's drama cycle. And they cycle around four times. I've learned this from my research over the past fifteen years. You have a thought followed by a feeling followed by a behavior. That's set number one. That last behavior invokes another thought about that last behavior, which is followed by a feeling, which is followed by a behavior. That's the second set. In the third set, you have another thought about the last behavior, which invokes another feeling, which produces another behavior. Now we're at the last cycle, which does the same thing: thought, feeling, behavior. And we're back to the starting point.

John: Each time, do you come back to that first thought?

Carol: Generally speaking, you will. Or you'll have a variation of that original thought. One woman said to me, "I discovered that my drama cycles have drama cycles."

John: At the end of the fourth cycle, what then? I noticed that you spoke of yours as ending with some variation on quit, avoid, go away, bail out, shut down. Is that how they all end?

Carol: Fight or flight. . . .

John: Say more please.

Carol: It's either fight or flight in some form, such as confront or quit, bail out, talk back or argue. You'll need to look to see what you do in your own drama cycle.

John: Can both be present?

Carol: Absolutely.

John: It would seem that the end result of fight or flight is really the same: get it over with. Is it the nature of the drama cycle to want it over with?

Carol: Yes. Interestingly enough, that intent doesn't get accomplished. We just go around and around and around like gerbils on those little treadmills. By trying to get out of it, we just get more deeply into it. We know when we're in it. Sometimes we even feel it coming on. It's in that moment when it's about to hit that we are truly at choice. I've seen it over and over again. People know it's coming and they do it anyway. If people would just stop and say, "Don't go there," they could stop the drama cycle anywhere, anytime.

John: It sounds compulsive—we see it coming and we go there anyway. Why do we do it?

Carol: Because *we're not playing big enough in our lives.* We really have a life purpose. Many of us don't know what that life purpose is. But you don't have to know what it is in order to play a bigger game. We play very small. We don't take on things to expand ourselves. Look at relationships, for example. In addition to promoting families and passing on traditions, a relationship is also designed to have us transcend our petty humanness and become the greatness in us. It's as if to say, "In this relationship I'm going to be the best that I can be. I'm going to welcome all the challenges that this person brings to me."

John: Carol, that's so obviously a higher level at which to be in relationship with other people. Why aren't we all doing that? Why are so willing to sit around in the same old complacent, unenlightened place?

Carol: I don't think we *all* are. Buckminster Fuller said there were four kinds of people in our world: those who are asleep, those who are stirring, those who are just awakening, and those who are awake. For the people who are asleep, who are going through life taking it as it comes and not making any waves, the most empowering thing we can do for them is to respect that and allow them to go their own way, and not to impose our principles on them. Now, we need to keep an eye on them because in their sleep they will cause wars and famine and other harmful things. We need to have the necessary structures in place so that they're contained as well as possible.

Then there's the group that is stirring. They're aware that there's more out there in life that they haven't been exposed to. They've not had the opportunities to "broaden their horizons" yet; for the most part, they're not going to do much about it. We are to respect them and let them be where they are also, rather than shaking them awake. Maybe this is not the time.

The third group of people is sitting up, rubbing their eyes, and saying, "Oh, look, it's daylight. Time to get up." Those are the people you want to partner with if you're going to do something. They're ready.

Then there's the group that's wide awake, saying, "Okay, let's get it together and go do something." They will help the rest of humanity stay as strong and healthy as possible.

We're in different places and at different levels. Empowered listening means really recognizing where people are, honoring them *exactly* where they are, and joining with people who are ready to make something happen. I spent a good five or six years early on in my work trying to wake up people who were sound asleep, and it was like hitting my head against a wall. I determined that it's a lot easier to work with people who are wide awake and ready to get something happening. By combining our efforts and our energies, we will bring the entire humanity up to another level.

John: I've noticed that there are more people today intent on having things change. Having things be better. Do you know where that's coming from?

Carol: People started doing personal work over twenty years ago. They were beginning to shift the listening about where we could be and how we could be as human beings. I now hear slogans on television that started twenty years ago. The U.S. Army: "Be all that you can be." I heard a politician say on CSPAN, "I want to work for a world that works for everybody."

The momentum of empowerment has started. I may not see the results of my work until 2020 or 2050. I'm clear that listening at some point is going to be the core to how we communicate, how we operate in the world, and no one will even remember who started it. Since I've begun being very committed to listening, people are sending me articles about listening from all over. When the critical mass happens, and I can count on that, it will take the rest of the people with it: those who are sleeping, those who are stirring, the ones who are almost awake, and the ones who are wide awake. That moment will take us all to the next level.

John: Certainly listening is proactive, but there's a technique that you employ to create an opportunity to listen. That's by asking questions, such as "How do you want me to communicate with you? How do you want to be listened to?" Say a little more about that.

Carol: You ask questions in a way that indicates genuine interest. I watched Virginia Satir many years ago. She was a well-known marriage and family counselor. She would ask questions that were so gentle and so direct. For example, when she was working with families, she would ask the youngest child—four or five years old—"When your brother Larry, who's twelve, says to you, 'You little punk kid, why don't you pick up your clothes?' how do you feel, Justin?" Justin would say, "I think he's a big bully." And she would say, "Justin, would it be possible that your brother loves you and that's the way he shows you that?" "Love me? By calling me a punk kid and telling me to pick up my clothes?" "Well, Justin, maybe Larry's just learning how to take care of a little brother. Maybe he doesn't know how. Do you think that's possible?" And this little kid would say, so surprised, "Really? He doesn't?" because of course to him a twelve-year-old brother was God. Virginia Satir would say, "Yes, maybe he doesn't know how to talk. Did you ever think about that, Justin?" All of a sudden, Larry got that Justin felt a certain way when he very carelessly said what he said. And he understood that maybe he didn't know much about little kids, but that was the best he could do at twelve.

I really admired the way she asked questions. Sometimes she'd say something like, "I know you have the answer and I'm certainly listening, so what do you think?" It was so natural to her. It was very clear that this woman was on to something. If you want people to really get how powerful they are, you ask with authenticity about them. You'll find out more about them.

I used to hate cocktail parties or coffee gatherings where I was expected to make small talk. Then I turned small talk into a research project, and now I love these gatherings. I find out more about people in five minutes than most people find out in a whole lifetime, because I ask questions. Not just the standard, "What do you do," like I'm sizing them up. I ask what they do with real interest. "Wow. How did you get into that? What led you to do that work?" I'm genuinely interested. I'm not pretending. When people get that you're interested in them, they will find you interesting. Which I always find to be an amazing phenomenon.

John: When I ask people what they do, and I'm curious enough to continue to ask questions, when I'm through they're almost compelled to reciprocate by asking, "And, John, what do you do?" to show an equal amount of interest. That can be very powerful when I'm talking to a potential business partner or customer.

Carol: Yes. You can use questions to shift the listening to what's possible. Virginia Satir did that. She never challenged, just asked questions and presented possibilities. Not right, not wrong. Is that possible? People's listening shifted in her presence.

Sometimes I ask someone, "Is it possible that your father loved you and the only way he knew how to show it was to just grunt when you said good morning? Maybe that's the only way he knew how to respond. Is that possible?" Well, yes, anything's possible. I've opened up the possibility and shifted the paradigm around.

John: By asking those kinds of questions and listening intently, you can change who people are—certainly at that moment.

Carol: Yes, you can.

John: Most people have a tremendous fear of being changed because it implies dominance and control. This is a much gentler, non-manipulative way to allow people to reach their own conclusions.

Carol: The only concern I have when people are asking ques-

111

tions is that they might turn it into a technique. Other people are smart. The minute you're doing this, rather than being present, they'll say, "Don't try that 'listening stuff' with me." When you've been listening and truly present, that's when the child, the wife, the husband, the partner, the employee, the CEO, has been really touched by your authenticity. And they will imitate that.

When you think you can do this on auto-pilot, you've just missed the boat. When you've integrated it and it becomes part of you, though, it's natural, not a technique. It's how you now behave. Empowered listening for me is now how I behave. When I first took it on, many years ago, I had to work at it. And life certainly provided me with enough challenges—it still does. The difference is that I work on it faster. Now it's in me.

There are times when I don't use empowered listening—for example, when I'm watching some of the talk shows. I'm really watching them to see what the listening is in our community. I have loud opinions about that. And since there's nobody else around, I have a great time talking back to the people on the television screen.

That doesn't happen a whole lot. I believe that empowered listening is not only worth disciplining yourself to have, it's a major discipline in empowering the whole world. I see 100 million people, by the year 2020, being masterful listeners.

John: It would be a different world.

Carol: Yes, it would. It would be wonderful for everyone to wake up and have somebody say, "How are you?" and stay with them for the answer.

In conclusion, I want to say it has been my intention, in this conversation, to get people to grasp that *everyone* is capable of being a masterful listener. Everyone! There is no person who's more capable than any other. It's something that we can all attain, and I'm out to recruit 100 million people as masterful listeners. My invitation is to come join me!

About the Author

Carol McCall has impacted the lives of more than two million people through her workshops, the companies with which she has worked, and numerous publications. She has dedicated her professional life to the development, training, and coaching of individuals and organizations in the area of personal growth and communication. She has more than thirty years of experience as an educator, therapist, business executive, consultant, coach, and successful entrepreneur.

She is the founder of the World Institute Group of Companies/Center for the Rights of Humanity, a pioneer in the field of life development. She is the creator and leader of the Empowerment of Listening Course and the co-creator of the Possibility of Women Workshop and the Relationships Course. She is also co-creator of the Design Your Life Workshop.

McCall is deeply committed to the empowerment of women. She believes that women, working together and in tandem with men, are powerful catalysts for social change. She co-created the Possibility of Women Workshop as a vehicle through which women can be awakened to their own inner but untapped resources, allowing them to become pro-active in bringing their gifts to the world for the good of humankind.

A graduate of Northwestern University, she holds a master's degree and is pursuing a doctoral degree in several academic areas. She is the creator of Life Development, a results-oriented, fast-paced, dynamic technology that allows the individual and/or business to discover and align values and vision with productivity and results that lead to natural success and bottom-line achievements. She is also in research, and training in communication psychology.

McCall is ardently pursuing a vision of having 100 million people who are masterful listeners by the year 2020 so that emerging generations will not be destined to repeat social patterns that lead to famine, war, poverty, child abuse, racism, and human degradation.

She is married, the mother of two grown very successful children, and a grandmother. Her son is a graduate of Dartmouth University and her daughter is a University of California—Davis graduate. She passionately honors her values of sunshine and warm weather by living with her husband in Scottsdale, Arizona, and Montego Bay on the Island of Jamaica.

This book has been adapted from "The Empowerment of Listening" audio tape in which she was interviewed by her colleague John Fogg. More than 50,000 people have already listened to the tape.